Easy Banjo Songbook

with Video & Audio Access

Revised Edition

by
Geoff Hohwald

Copyright 2021 by Watch & Learn, Inc./ Geoff Hohwald, 2nd Edition
ALL RIGHTS RESERVED. Any copying, arranging, or adapting of this work without the consent of the owner is an infringement of copyright.

The *Easy Banjo Songbook Package* combines the following three resources:

The Book

The *Easy Banjo Songbook* contains helpful hints on learning to play the 5 string banjo. It also contains all of the written music or tablature for each of the songs taught in this course, including right and left hand fingering, measure numbers, and chord symbols. The chord symbols are included to let the guitar know what chords to play when accompanying the banjo.

Note: The On-Screen tablature on the Video is designed as a reference to let you know where you are in the song and does not include fingering. If you need to know fingerings or measure numbers, look at the included tablature in the book.

Online Video Access

The *Easy Banjo Songbook Video* plays and explains every measure of each song and then plays song exercises at 3 different slow speeds. Once learned, the student plays the chosen song at 3 different slow speeds to burn the song in. The tablature for each song is displayed on screen in large, easy-to-read tablature. If you need fingering or measure numbers, you can reference the included book.

To watch the video lessons on your smart phone, tablet, or computer, go to the following address on the web:

cvls.com/extras/ebs

Online Audio Tracks

The *Easy Banjo Songbook Package* includes online access to full band, play-along tracks that play each song at 3 faster speeds, two of which are faster than the Video. This helps the student perfect their timing and get used to playing with others. These are similar to the other beginning/intermediate *BanjoCompass.com* products that include several speeds on the Video and also full band play-along tracks (*Banjo Primer Deluxe Edition,* and *Easy Gospel Songs*).

The Downloadable Audio Tracks are available at the following address on the web:

cvls.com/extras/ebs

Table Of Contents

	Page
Banjo Primer Learning System	4-5
About the Instructor	6
Section 1 - Getting Started	7
Tuning the Banjo	8-9
Tablature	10-12
The Picks	13
Section 2 - The Songs	14
Cumberland Gap	15
Wildwood Flower	16-17
Sally Gooden	18
8th of January	19
Will the Circle Be Unbroken	20-21
Old Joe Clark	22-23
Whiskey Before Breakfast	24
Soldier's Joy	25
Devil's Dream	26-27
Bury Me Beneath the Willows	28-29
Little Maggie	30-31
Tom Dooley	32-33
Salty Dog	34-35
Train 45	36-37
Sourwood Mountain	37
Reuben's Train	38
Home Sweet Home	39
Arkansas Traveler	40-41
Dueling Banjos	42-51

The Banjo Primer Learning System

The *Banjo Primer Learning System* consists of four integrated Book/Video/Audio Track packages designed to start the raw beginner correctly in playing the 5 string banjo and establish a firm foundation leading to years of enjoyment. The courses are as follows:

Beginning Banjo Warm-Up Series with Online Video & Audio is designed to get the absolute beginner physically ready for the *Banjo Primer Deluxe Edition*. It will help the student train the right hand to perform with the speed and accuracy that is essential to playing the 5 string Banjo. Developing the right hand will pay big dividends in the future. Geoff will guide you by using a simple forward roll pattern at gradually increasing speeds to relax and strengthen the right hand. It is recommended that the student use this method 15 minutes per day for the first 4 weeks as part of their practice.

Banjo Primer Deluxe Edition Book/DVD/CD is the instruction part of the *Banjo Primer Learning System*. It incorporates a step-by-step teaching system that took over forty years to develop and has been used by over 200,000 students ranging in age from 6 to 85 years old. It combines a proven sequence of learning with play-along DVD or online video exercises that move at a gradual pace. First, each song is divided into exercises and practiced along with the video at gradually increasing speeds. Once mastered, the exercises become a song. This enables them to not only hear what it is supposed to sound like but to see the correct hand and finger movements. As soon as the student works through the video, they can then practice with full band play-along tracks to prepare them for playing with others. Songs taught are *Boil Them Cabbage Down, Shady Grove, Worried Man Blues, Cripple Creek, Basic Breakdown, John Hardy, Black Mountain Rag, Kicking Mule, & Little Maggie.*

Easy Banjo Songbook with Online Video & Audio by Geoff Hohwald is the next step in the *Banjo Primer Learning System* teaching 19 new songs. Just like the *Banjo Primer,* we start with video instruction. Once each song is memorized, we use the included 55 play-along tracks to let the student play each song along with a bluegrass band at gradually increasing speeds. Each song is carefully written at the same difficulty enabling the student to learn new songs quickly. Includes over four hours of video instruction. Songs included are *Cumberland Gap, Wildwood Flower, Sally Gooden, 8th of January, Will the Circle be Unbroken, Old Joe Clark, Whiskey Before Breakfast, Soldier's Joy, Devil's Dream, Bury Me Beneath the Willows, Little Maggie, Tom Dooley, Salty Dog, Train 45, Sourwood Mountain, Rueben's Train, Home Sweet Home, Arkansas Traveler, & Dueling Banjos.*

Easy Banjo Gospel Songs with Online Video & Audio is the gospel equivalent to *Easy Banjo Songbook.* It contains easy arrangements to 8 popular Gospel Songs that can be learned quickly. There are multiple play-along tracks at gradually increasing speeds for each song. The solos are arranged to enhance the melody so as to convey the true feeling of each song. Songs include *Precious Memories, Do Lord, Crying Holy, Uncloudy Day, What a Friend We Have in Jesus, Amazing Grace, I Am A Pilgrim, & Swing Low Sweet Chariot.*

These products are available at your local music store, on Amazon.com, or call 800-416-7088. You can also check out our website at BanjoCompass.com.

Watch & Learn, Inc.
2947 East Point St
East Point, GA 30344
800-416-7088
sales@watchlearn.com

About the Instructor

Geoff Hohwald began playing banjo in 1963 in Columbus, Ohio which was a "hot bed of bluegrass" at the time. While there Geoff studied banjo under John Hickman. He performed with many other great musicians there including Bill Monroe's last two guitar players Tom Ewing and Wayne Lewis. Other Musicians that Geoff played with in the Columbus area were Red Allen, Sandy Rothman, Sid Campbell, Dave Evans, Frank Wakefield, Hylo Brown, Buddy Thomas, The Fields Brothers, Landon Messer, Earl Taylor and Brian Aldridge.

Since coming to Atlanta, Geoff has played with Bear Creek in Underground Atlanta, at the Alliance Theatre for the Robber Bridegroom, with the Atlanta Pops Orchestra, and is one of the founding members of the Greater Atlanta Bluegrass Band.

Geoff is mostly known around the country for his banjo teaching materials which are sold world wide including the popular *Banjo Primer Deluxe Edition*. He currently teaches week long classes at John C. Campbell Folk School in Brasstown, North Carolina and at his home in Dahlonega, Georgia.

For information on week long banjo classes or individual instruction, contact Geoff at geoff@cvls.com.

Photo by John Crawford

Jam Class - John C. Campbell Folk School
Brasstown, NC

Section 1
Getting Started

Tuning the Banjo

Before playing the banjo, it must be tuned to standard pitch. If you have a piano at home, it can be used as a tuning source. The following diagram shows how to tune the open strings on the banjo to the piano.

Note - If your piano hasn't been tuned recently, the banjo may not agree perfectly with a pitch pipe or tuning fork. Some older pianos are tuned a half step below standard.

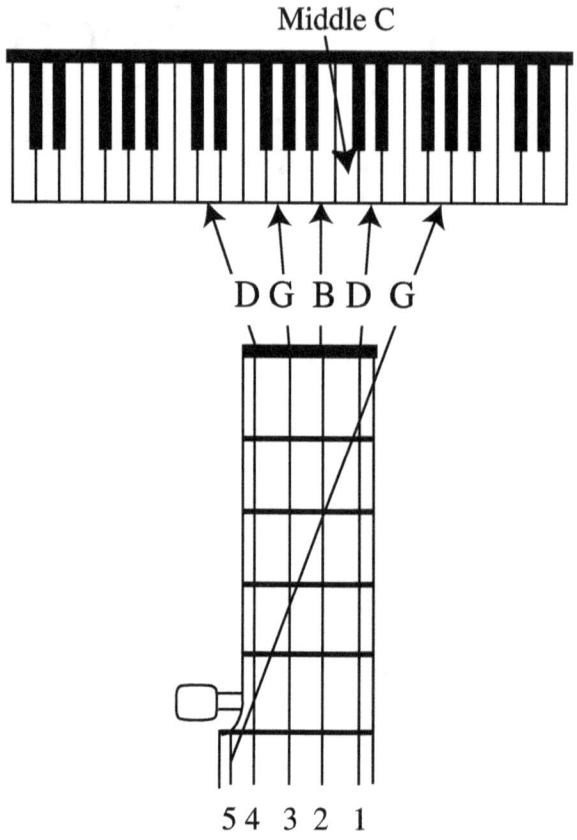

Website

If you need help with tuning your banjo, watch the free video lesson on tuning at our website. If you need additional assistance with tuning, take your banjo to your local music store and ask them to show you how to tune.

Electronic Tuner

If you can afford one, an electronic tuner is the fastest and most accurate way to tune a banjo. I highly recommend getting one. They are available for $20 - $30. You can even get an app for your phone to tune with.

Relative Tuning

Relative tuning is used to tune the banjo to itself when you don't have an electronic tuner.

1. Tune the 4th string to a D using a pitch pipe or other source.

2. Note the 4th string at the 5th fret. Tune the 3rd string until it sounds like the 4th string at the 5th fret.

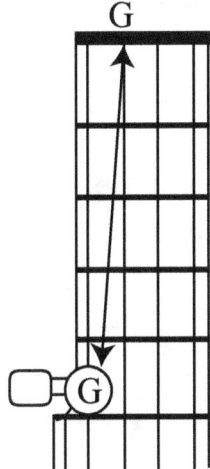

3. Note the 3rd string at the 4th fret. Tune the 2nd string until it sounds like the 3rd string at the 4th fret.

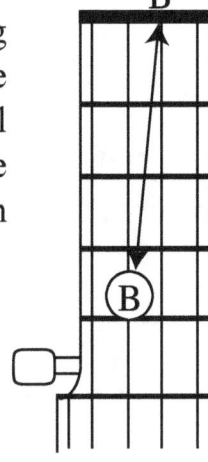

4. Note the 2nd string at the 3rd fret. Tune the 1st string until it sounds like the 2nd string at the 3rd fret.

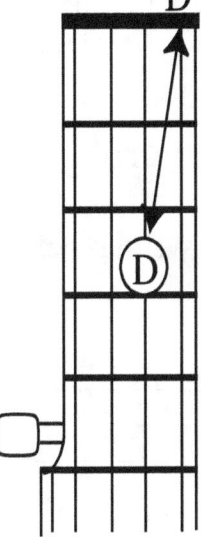

5. Note the 1st string at the 5th fret. Tune the 5th string until it sounds like the 1st string at the 5th fret.

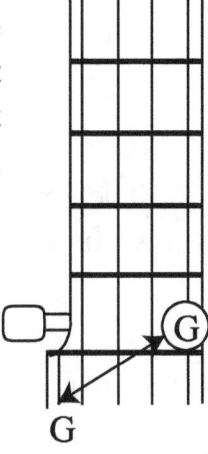

Tablature

Tablature is a system for writing music which shows the proper string and fret to play as well as the correct fingers to use.

In banjo tablature, each line represents a string on the banjo:

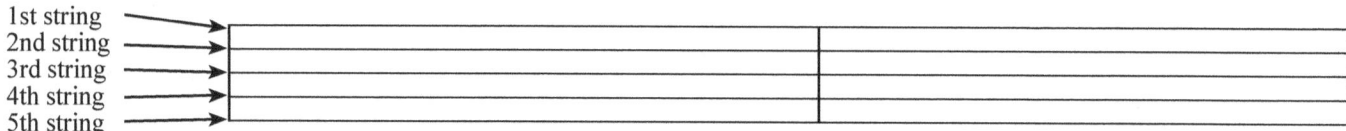

If the string is to be fretted, the fret number is written in the appropriate space, otherwise an (0) is written. Here are several examples:

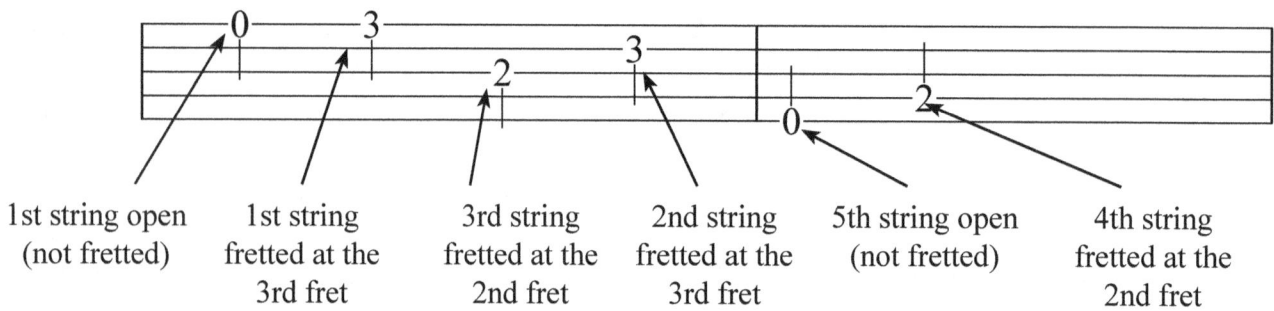

1st string open (not fretted)
1st string fretted at the 3rd fret
3rd string fretted at the 2nd fret
2nd string fretted at the 3rd fret
5th string open (not fretted)
4th string fretted at the 2nd fret

Right Hand Fingering

The correct finger of the right hand is written below the lines as shown below:

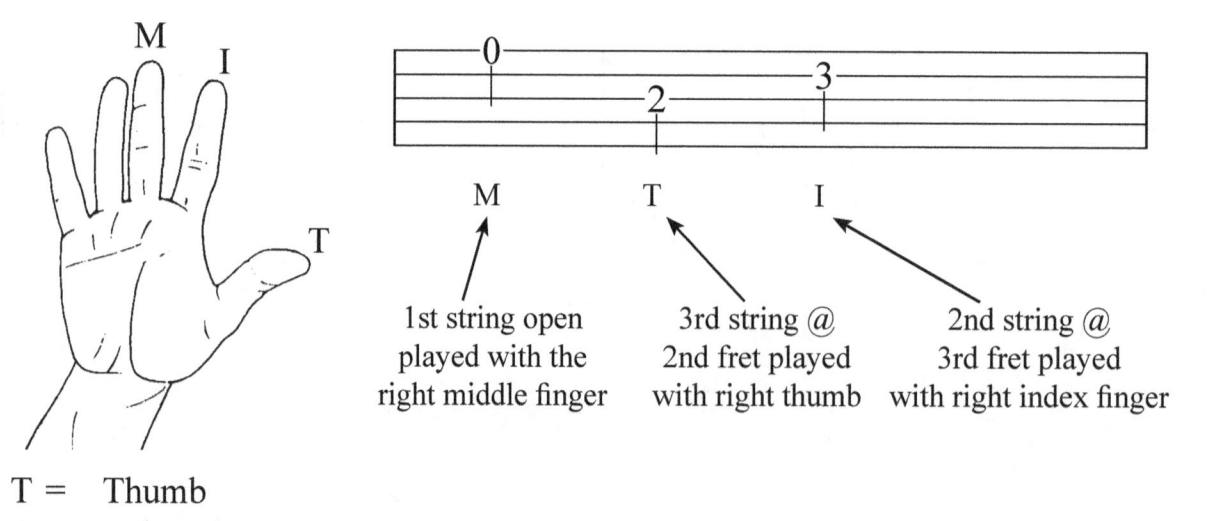

1st string open played with the right middle finger
3rd string @ 2nd fret played with right thumb
2nd string @ 3rd fret played with right index finger

T = Thumb
I = Index Finger
M = Middle Finger

10

Left Hand Fingering

Fingering is also written above the tablature. These are the recommended left hand fingerings for certain passages as shown below:

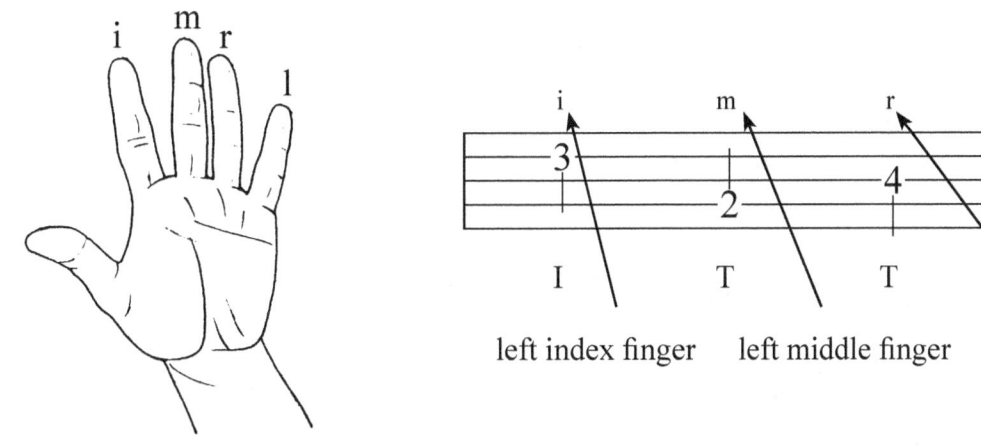

i = Index Finger
m = Middle Finger
r = Ring Finger
l = Little Finger

Hammer-on, Slide, Pull-off, Choke

The notation for hammer-on, pull-off, slide, and choke is shown as follows:

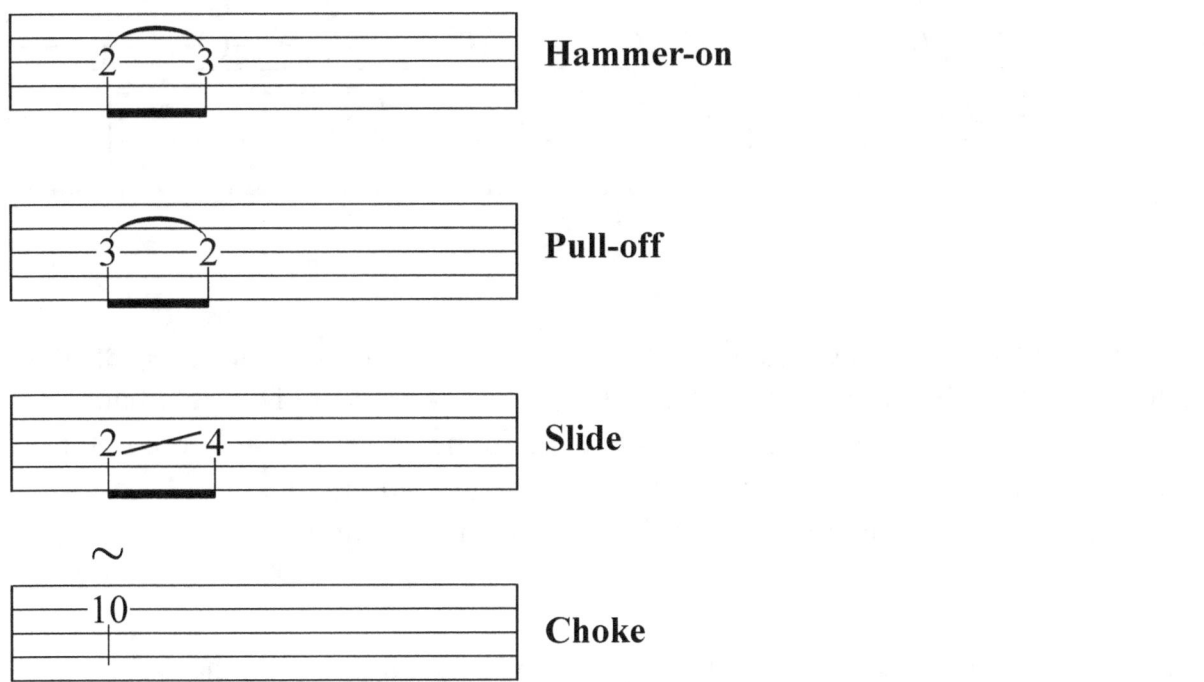

11

Timing

Musical notes are divided into equal time segments called rhythms. In this example, there are 4 beats per measure and each is divided in half. Each line represents 1/2 beat (eighth note).

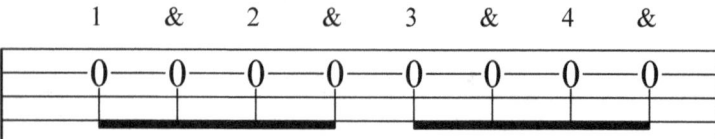

Most notes in this book are held for either 1 or 1/2 beat.

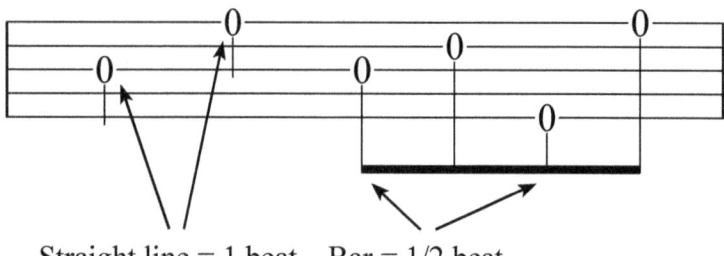

Straight line = 1 beat   Bar = 1/2 beat

Just count out the appropriate value for each note (1/2 beat or 1 beat).

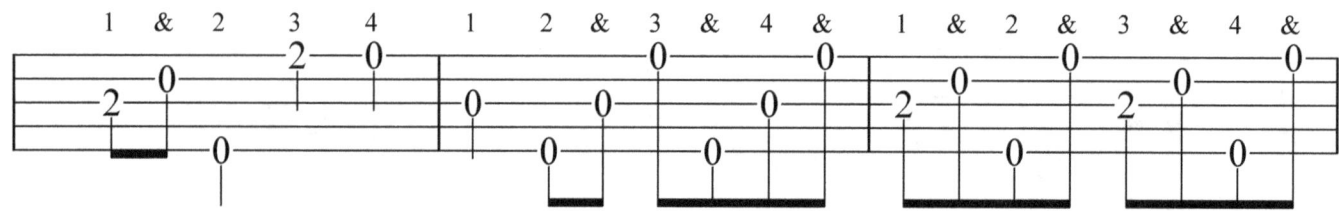

Note - As you work through the songs and exercises in this course, pay special attention to the right hand fingering and memorize it accurately. The right hand fingering is written in the book, but not included in the on-screen tablature in the video. This will train you to watch the instructor's right and left hands. Of course, you can always refer back to the book if you have any questions.

The Video and Audio Tracks are available at the following address on the web:

cvls.com/extras/ebs

THE PICKS

Two metal finger picks and a plastic thumb pick are used to play the banjo. Jim Dunlop metal finger picks (.025 & .0225) are recommended.

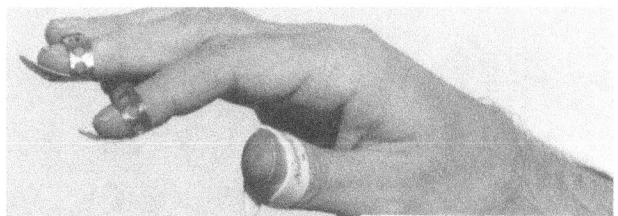

When placing the picks on your fingers, remember the following:
1. The finger picks are placed so they cover the front of the finger.
2. The picks extend about 1/8 inch beyond the front of the finger.
3. You may bend the sides of the picks, but do not bend the front.

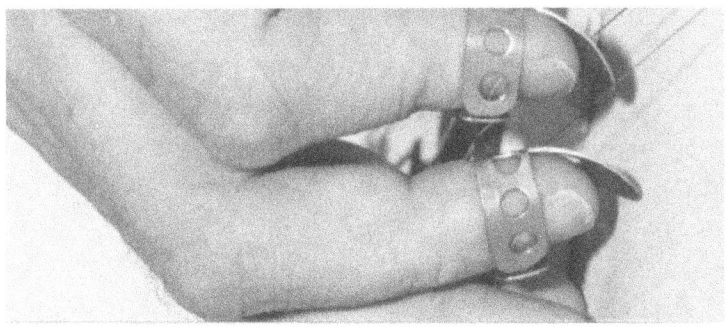

RIGHT HAND POSITION

Anchor the right hand on the banjo head with the little and ring finger.

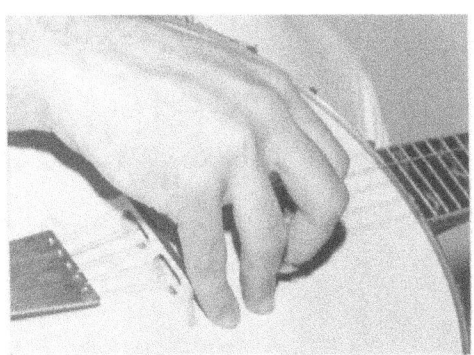 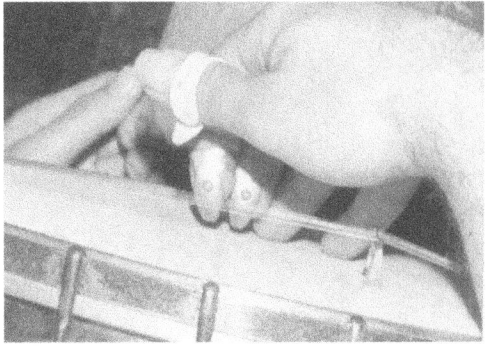

If you are a beginner and cannot use both the ring and little finger, it is okay to use one or the other until your hand strengthens.

Section 2
The Songs

Cumberland Gap

Traditional

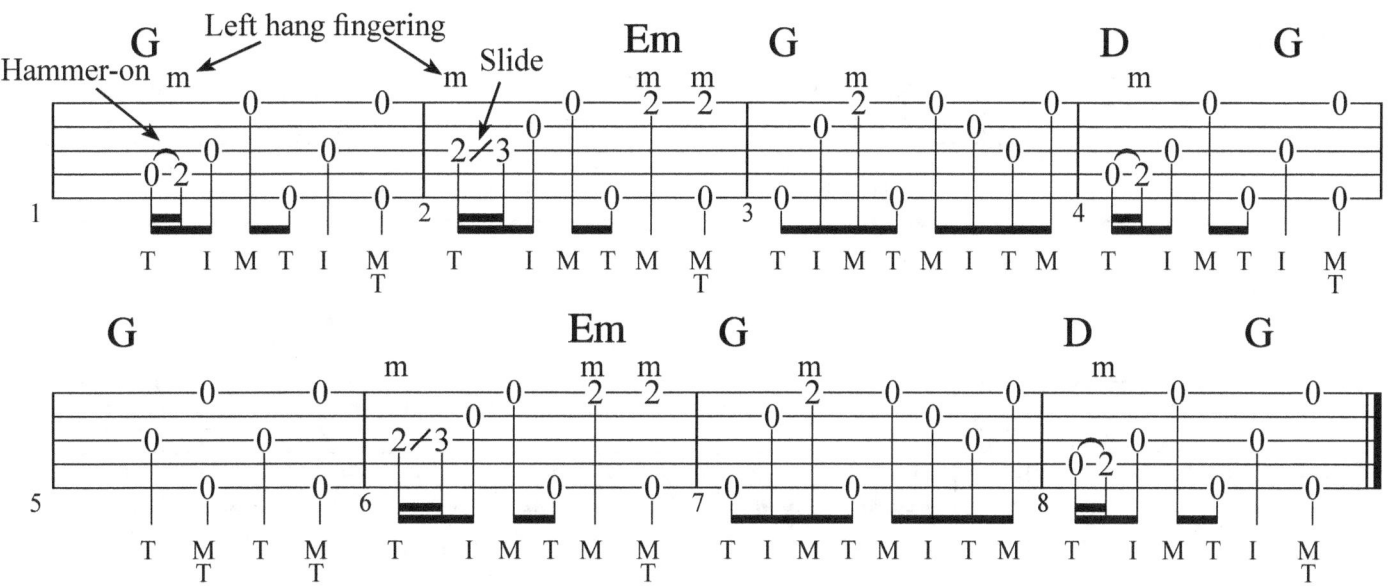

How To Learn A Song

1. Divide each song into individual measures and focus on them.
2. Listen to each measure on the Video several times before picking up the banjo to get the timing and accent in your mind. Then look at the tablature in this book and touch each note with your finger to make sure you focus on the notes and the correct fingers to use.
3. Now pick up the banjo and play the measure one note at a time. Try to play each note perfectly the first time.
4. Now play the measure slowly a few times. Once you can do this, play the measure perfectly five times in a row without making a mistake. This will take a lot of concentration. If you make a mistake, start over. Then make sure you can play the measure without looking at the tablature.
5. Once you have completed steps 1-4, play along with the Video at the slowest speed. Once mastered, proceed to the next speed. Once you can play all of the measures correctly, then put them together to make a song and practice the song along with the Video.
6. Once you can play the song at the fastest speed on the Video from memory, go to the downloadable audio tracks and practice with the band at gradually increasing speeds. Look for any measures that are difficult and isolate and practice them.
7. Most of all, relax and have fun.

Wildwood Flower

Traditional

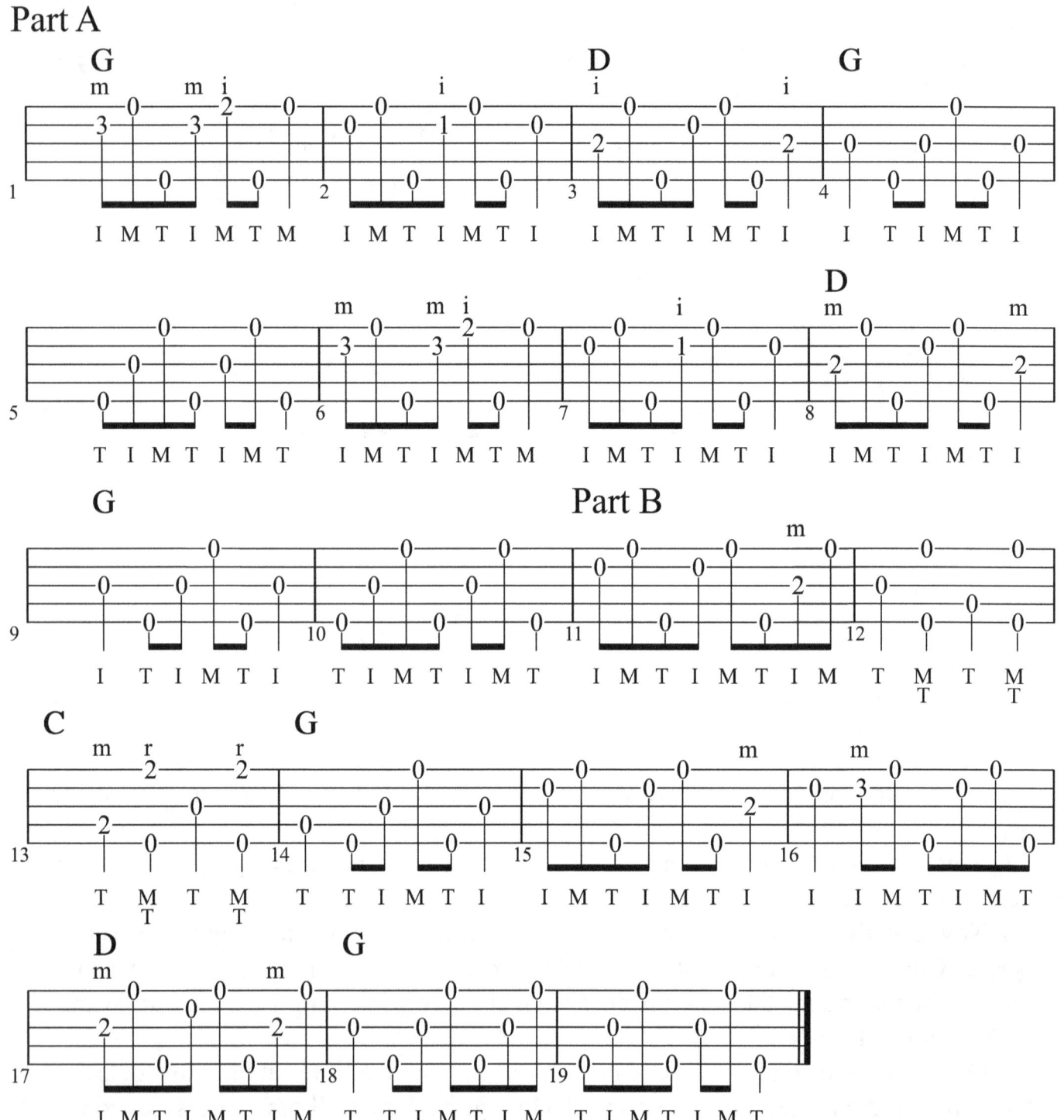

Note: From this point on, several songs in this book have a lyric page with melody line, chord progression, complete lyrics, and a discography of popular recordings of the song. You can use this information for singing the song and performing with a band. The other songs are commonly played as instrumentals so no lyrics are included. The lyric page for *Wildwood Flower* is on the following page.

Wildwood Flower

Traditional

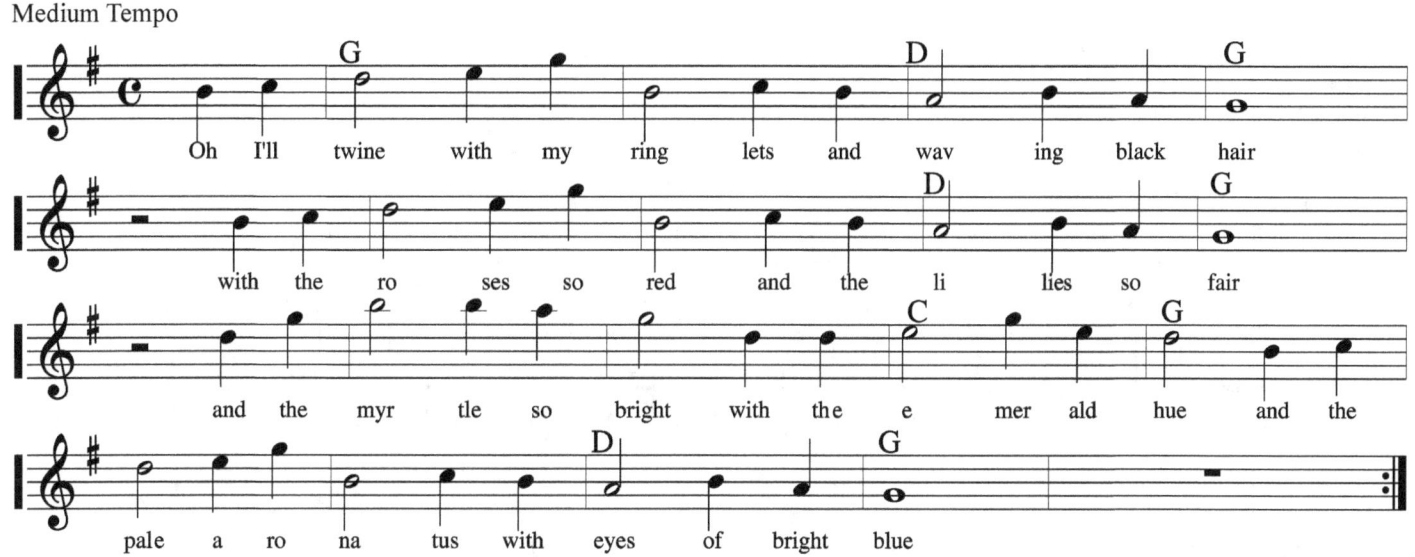

Oh, G I'll twine with my ringlets and wa D ving black hai G. r
With the roses so red and th D e lilies s G o fair
And the myrtle so bright with the e C merald hu G e
The pale aronatus with ey D es of bright blu G e

I will dance, I will sing, and my life shall be gay
I will charm every heart and his crown I will sway
When I woke from my dream and my idols of clay
Our portion of love had all gone away

Oh, he taught me to love him and promise to love
Through ill and misfortune all others above
How my heart is now wondering no misery can tell
He's left me no warning, no word of farewell

Oh, he taught me to love him, he called me his flower
That was blooming to cheer him through life's dreary hour
Oh, I longed to see him and regret the dark hour
He's gone and neglected this pale wildwood flower

Sally Gooden

Traditional

Most people play this in the key of A.
Capo at the 2nd fret to play in the key of A.

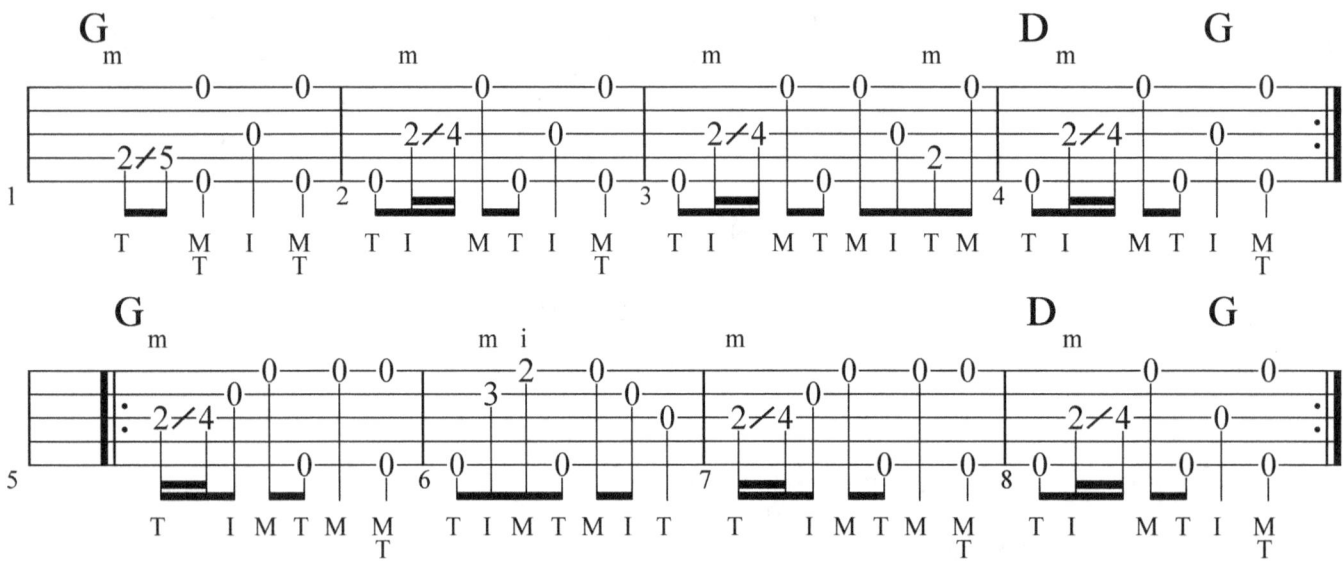

The Video and Audio Tracks are available at the following address on the web:
cvls.com/extras/ebs

Geoff playing the Wade Mainer banjo

8th of January

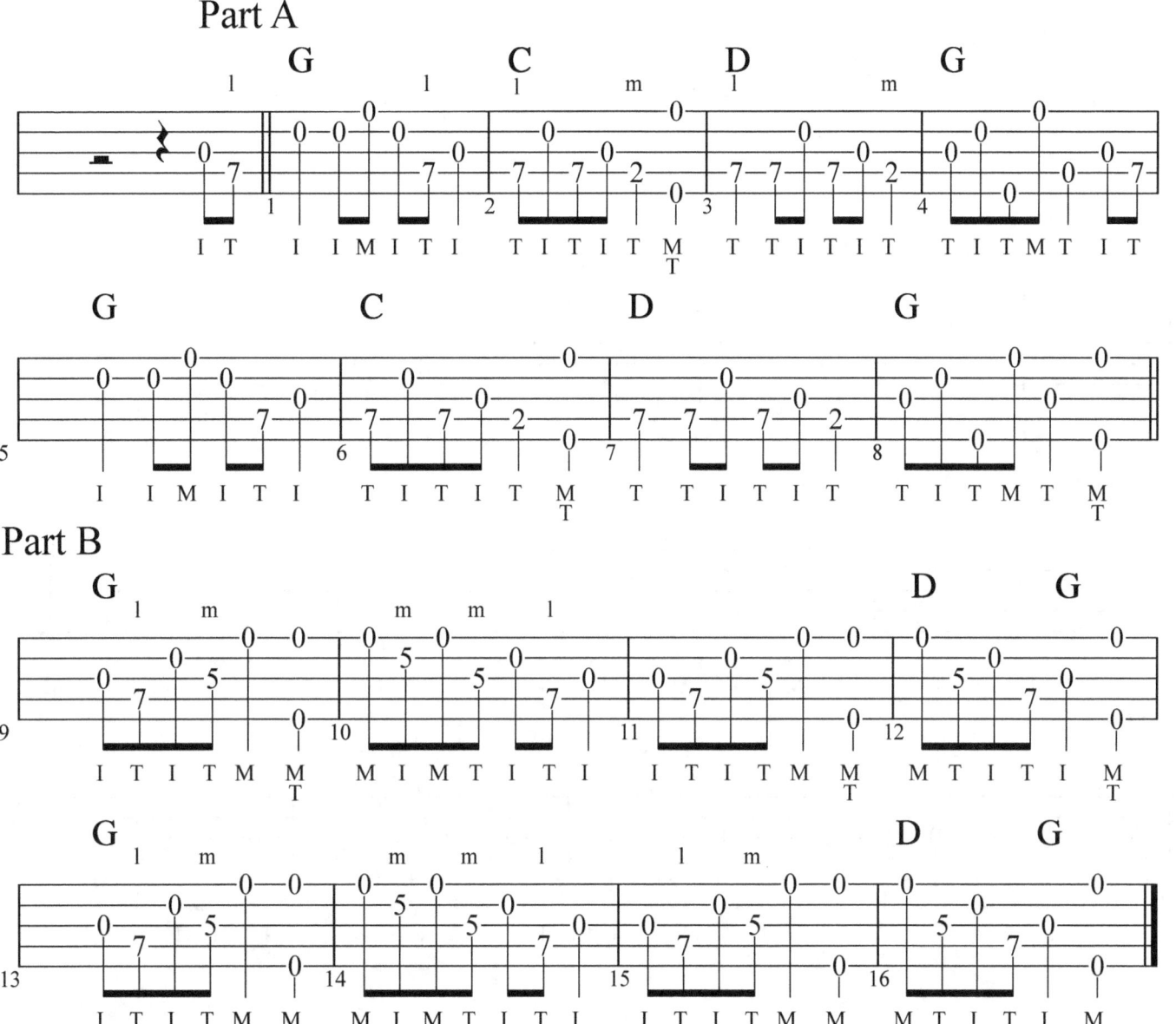

Will the Circle Be Unbroken

Traditional

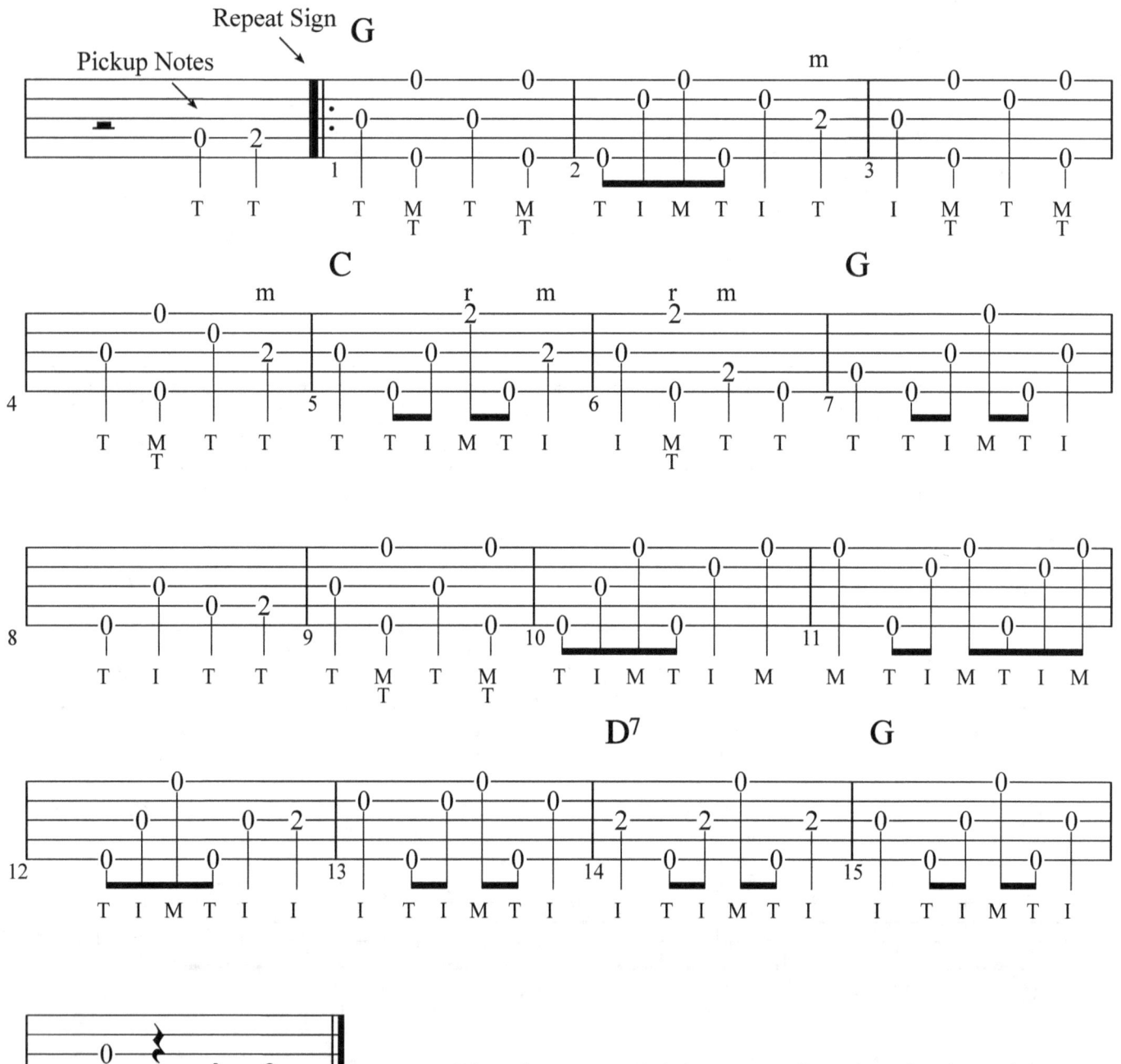

Play these two "pickup notes" and go back to the repeat sign if you want to play the song more than once.

Note: You will notice that when playing the 2nd & 3rd strings, I sometimes use the right index and sometimes the right thumb to play the string. Either is correct.

Will The Circle Be Unbroken

Traditional

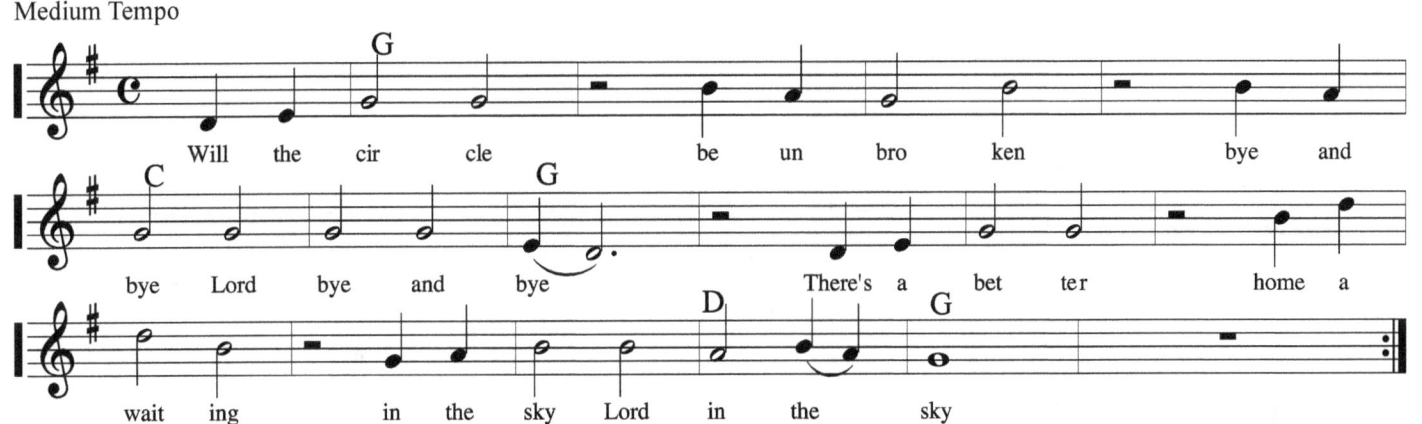

Chorus

I was standing by my window
On one cold and cloudy day
When I saw that hearse come rolling
For to carry my Mother away

Will the circle be unbroken
By and by, Lord, by and by
There's a better home a waiting
In the sky, Lord, in the sky

Well, I told that undertaker
Undertaker please drive slow
For this body you are hauling
Lord, I hate to see it go
Chorus

I will follow close behind her
Try to hold on and be brave
But I could not hide my sorrow
When they laid her in her grave
Chorus

I went back home, Lord, home was lonesome
Miss my Mother she was gone
All my brothers, sisters crying
What a home so sad and alone
Chorus

Nitty Gritty Dirt Band / Will The Circle Be Unbroken
Ralph Stanley / Songs My Mother Taught Me And More
Joan Baez / Greatest Hits

Old Joe Clark

Traditional

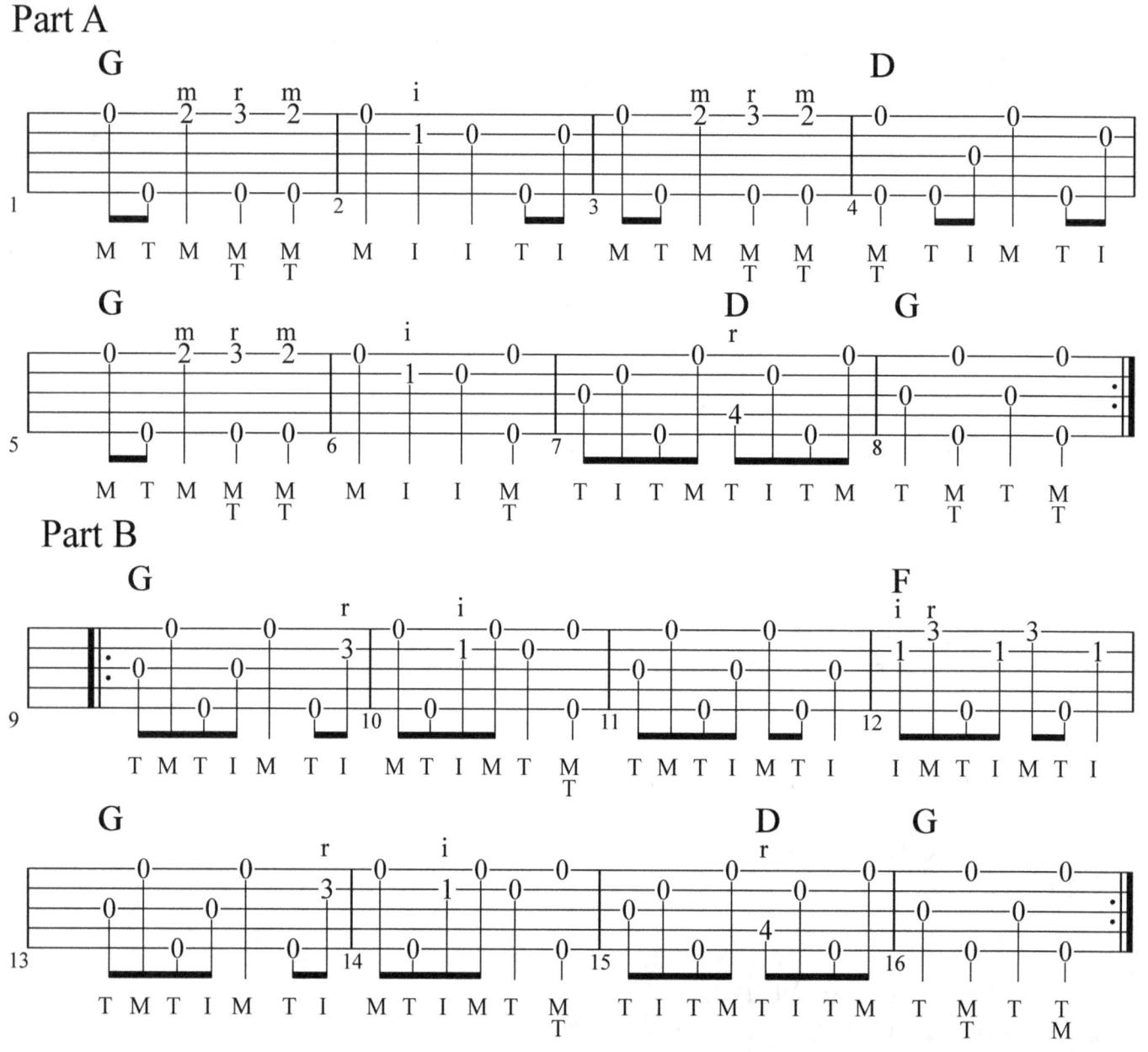

The Video and Audio Tracks are available at the following address on the web:

cvls.com/extras/ebs

Old Joe Clark

Traditional

Up Tempo

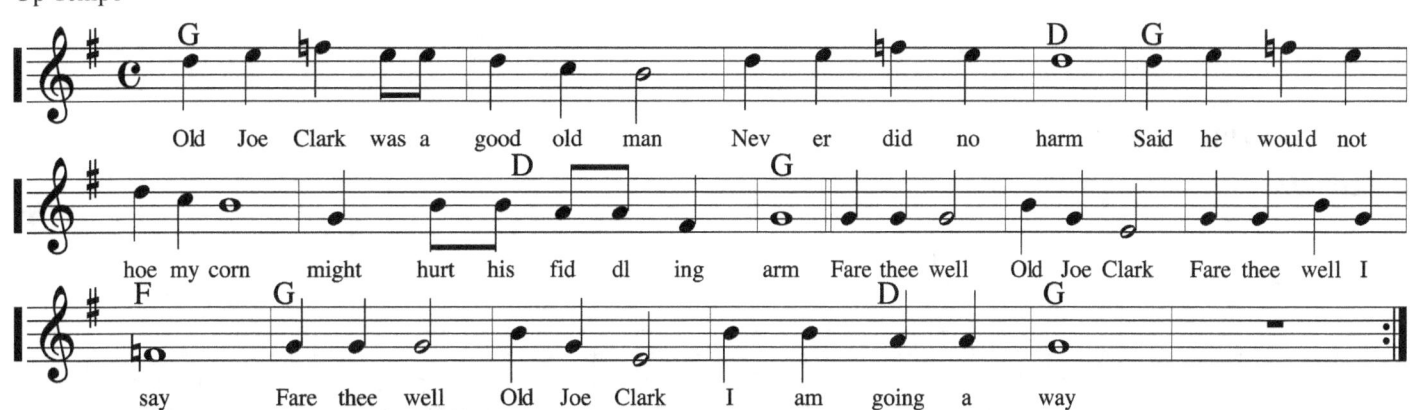

Old Joe Clark was a good old man / Never did no harm / Said he would not hoe my corn / might hurt his fiddling arm / Fare thee well Old Joe Clark / Fare thee well I say / Fare thee well Old Joe Clark / I am going away

Old Joe Clark was a good old man
Never did no harm
Said he would not hoe my corn
Might hurt his fiddling arm

Chorus
Fare thee well Old Joe Clark
Fare thee well I say
Fare thee well Old Joe Clark
I am going away

I went down to Old Joe's house
Never been there before
He slept on a feather bed
And I slept on the floor
Chorus

I went down to Old Joe's house
Old Joe wasn't home
Ate up all of Old Joe's meat
And left Old Joe the bone
Chorus

I went down to Old Joe's house
He invited me to supper
Stumped my toe on a table leg
And stuck my nose in the butter
Chorus

The Dillards / Homecoming And Family Reunion
Goose Island Ramblers / Best of the Goose Island Ramblers
Doc and Merle Watson / Home Sweet Home

Whiskey Before Breakfast

Traditional

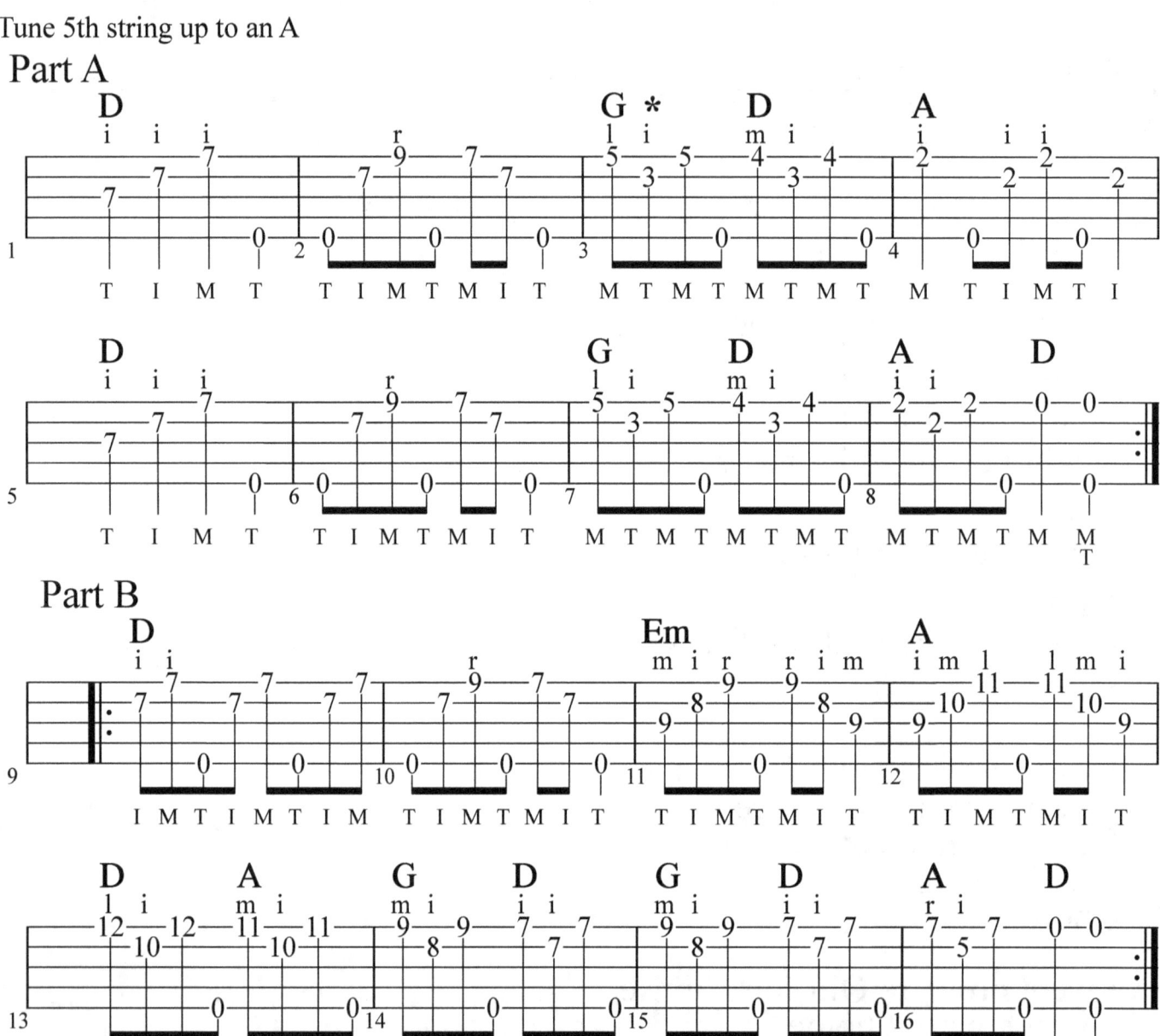

* **Note**: One of the themes of this course is that the 2nd and 3rd strings can be played with either the right thumb or right index finger. You will notice this when I play a song on the Video and alternate fingers depending on the speed. When you first learn the song, I recommend that you use the finger written in the tablature. As you play it more and more, you may use alternate fingers.

Soldier's Joy

Traditional

Tune 5th string to A

Part A

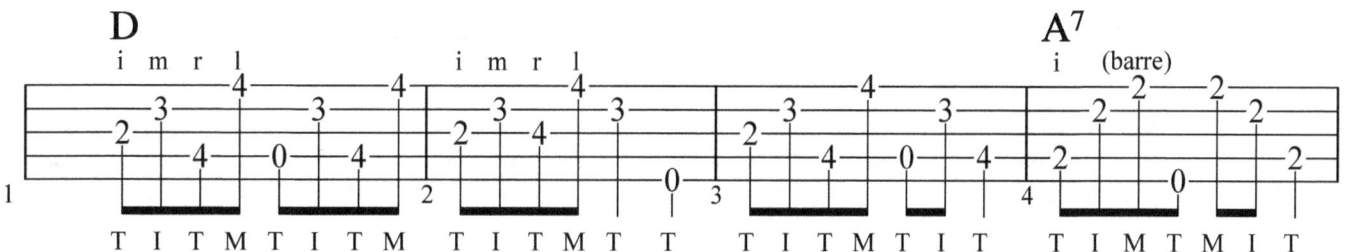
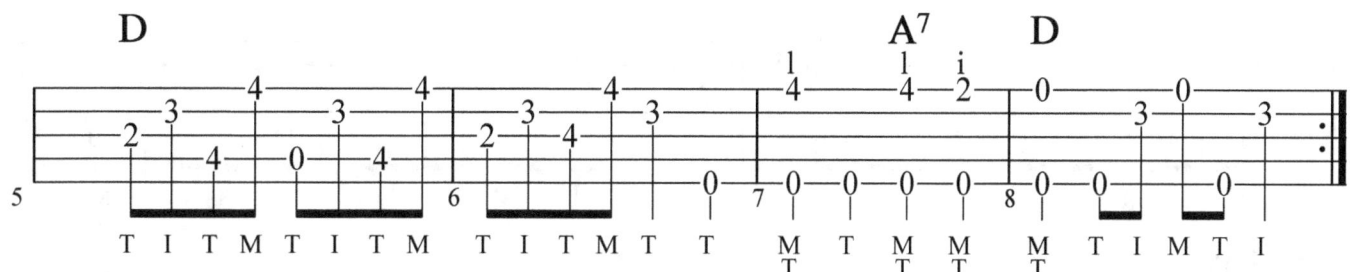

Part B

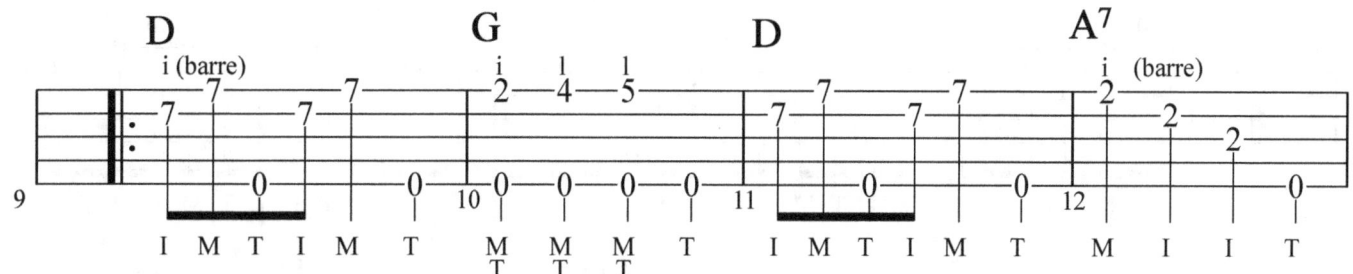
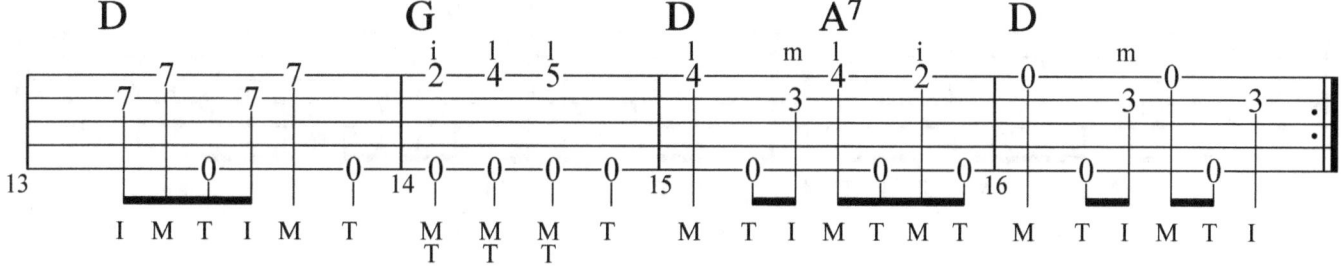

Devil's Dream

Traditional

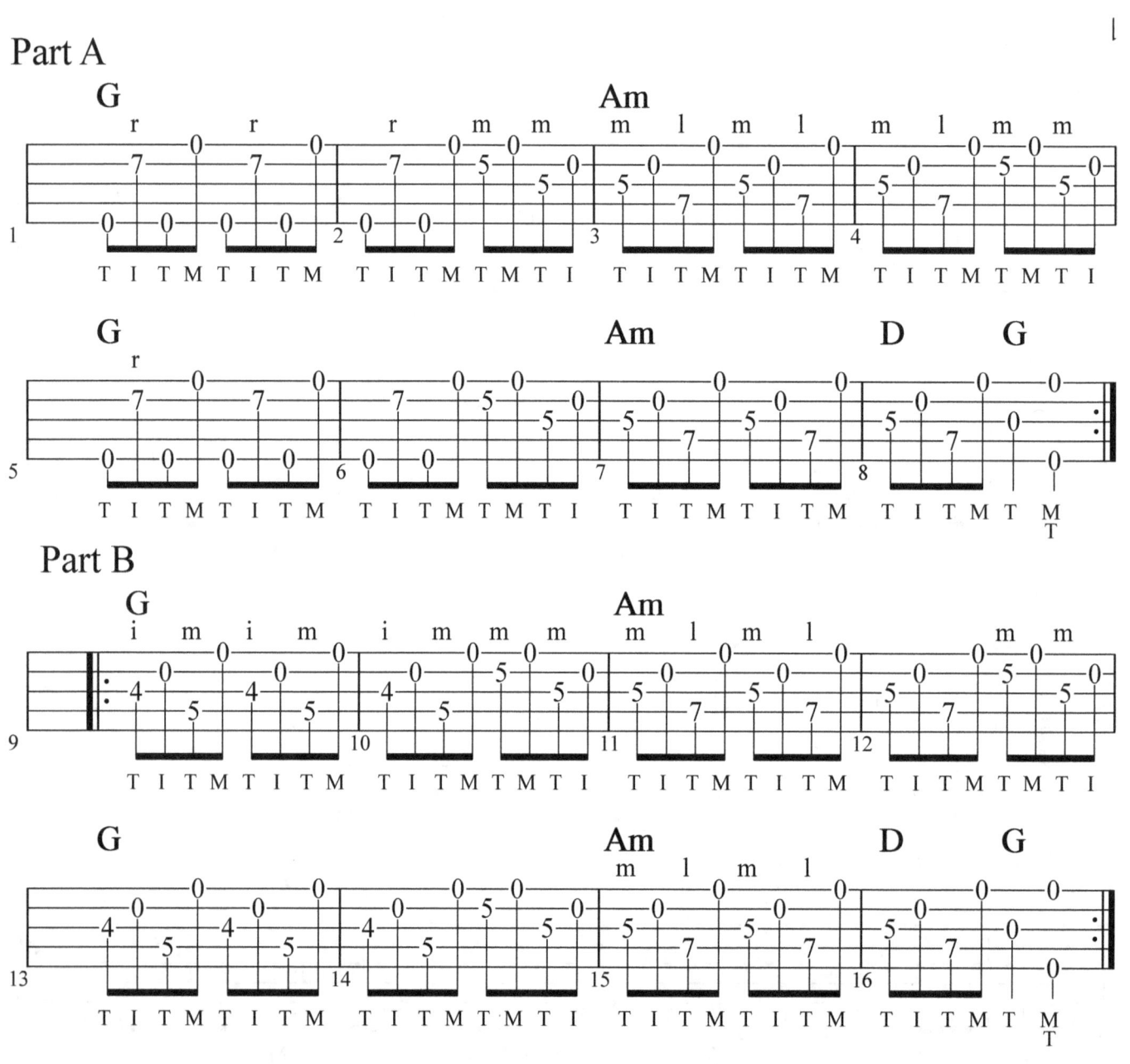

Note - Left hand fingering for *Devil's Dream* is on the following page.

Left Hand Fingering For Devil's Dream

Note: There are two ways to finger the music in measures 3-4, 7-8, 11-12, and 15-16:

1. Example 1 with the left hand using the index/ring finger combination.
2. Example 2 with the left hand using the middle/little finger combination.

Try both and see which is the most comfortable to you.

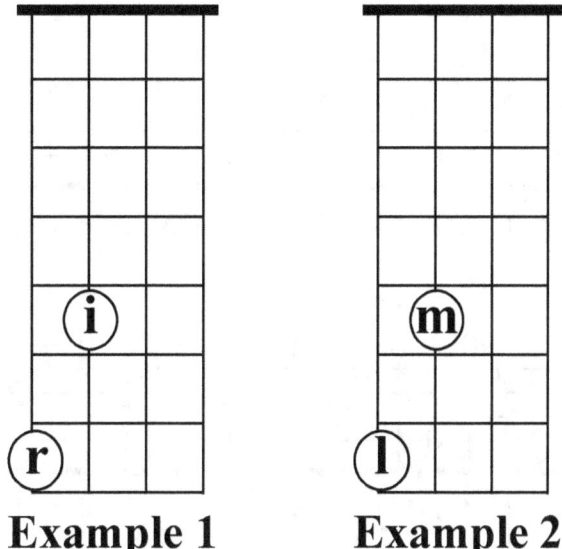

Example 1   **Example 2**

Forward-Backward Roll

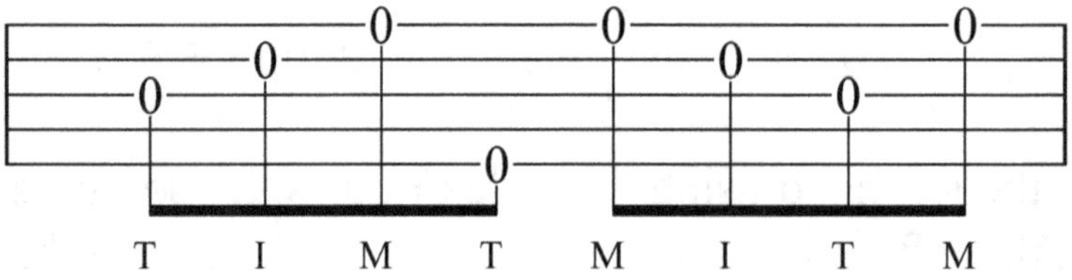

Bury Me Beneath the Willows

Traditional

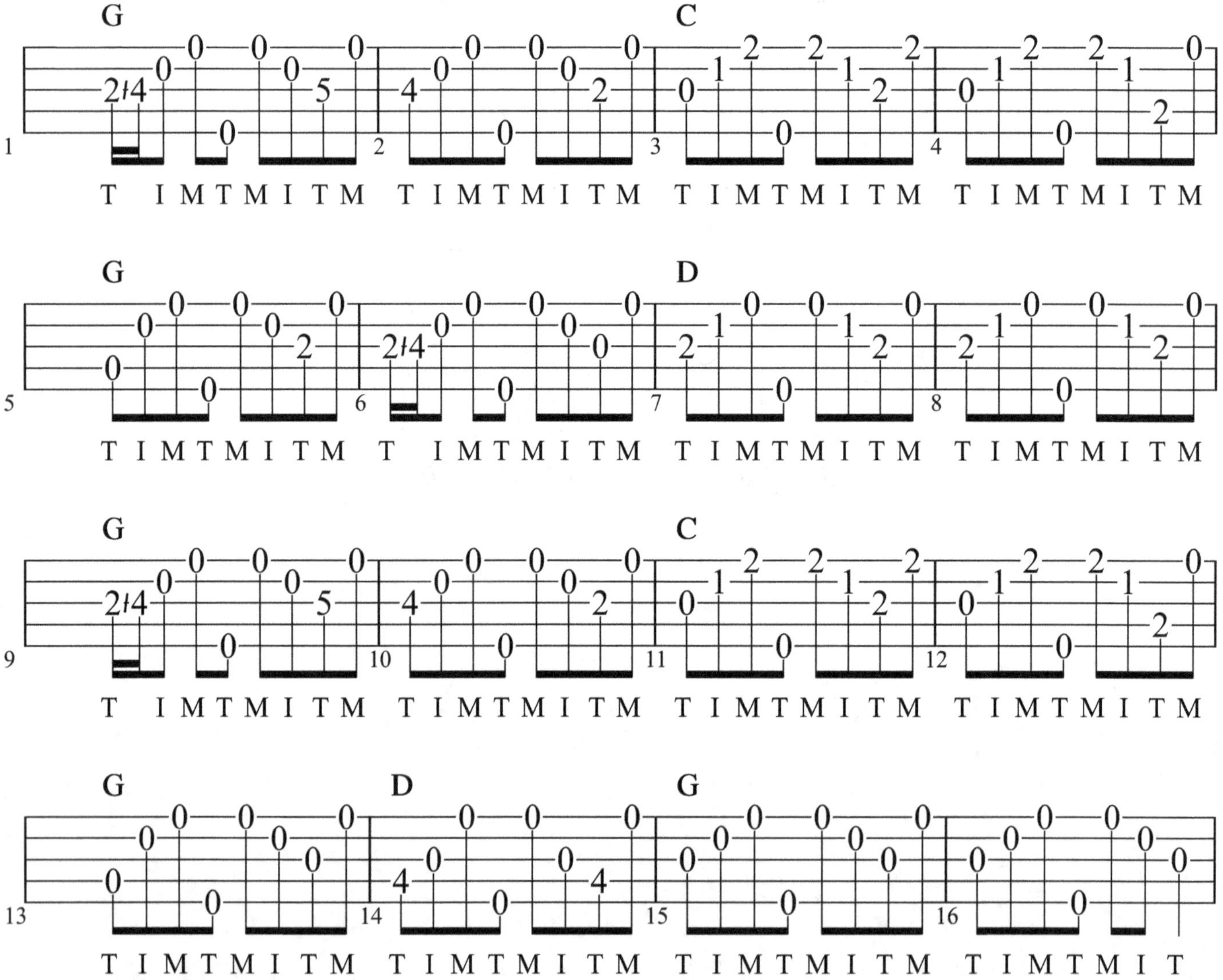

Bury Me Beneath the Willows

Traditional

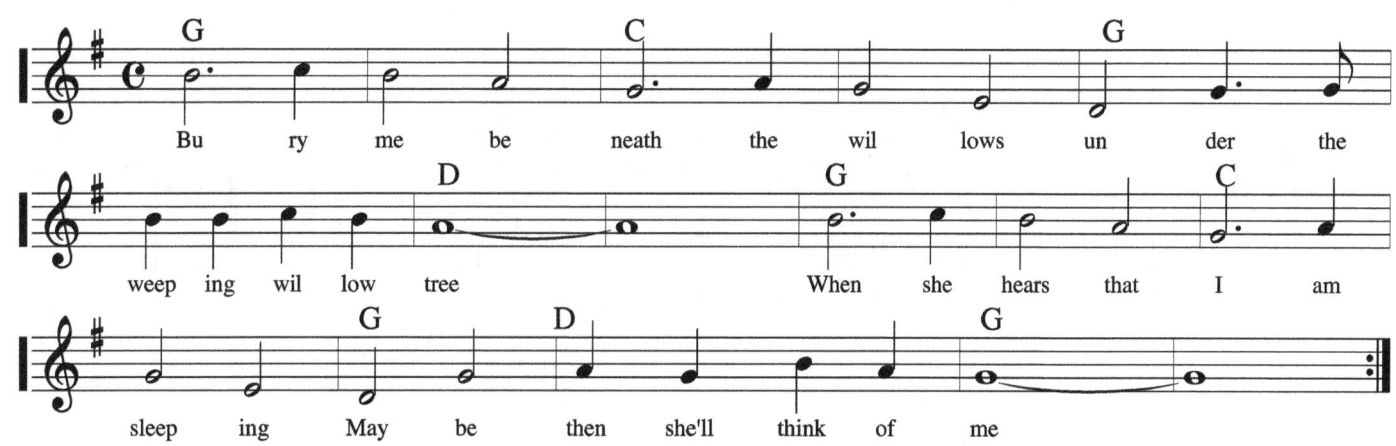

Chorus

G   C
Bury me beneath the willows
G   D
Under the weeping willow tree
G   C
When she hears that I am sleeping
G   D   G
Maybe then she'll think of me

My heart is sad and I'm in sorrow
Weeping for the one I love
When shall I see her, oh, no never
Till we meet in Heaven above

Tomorrow was to be our wedding
But Lord, oh Lord, where can she be?
She's gone, she's gone to find another
She no longer cares for me

She told me that she did not love me
I couldn't believe it was true
Until an angel softly whispered,
"She no longer cares for you".

Place on my grave a snow white lily
To prove my love for her was true
To show the world I died of grieving
For her love I could not win

Ricky Skaggs & Tony Rice / Skaggs & Rice
Monroe Brothers / Feast Here Tonight

Little Maggie

Traditional

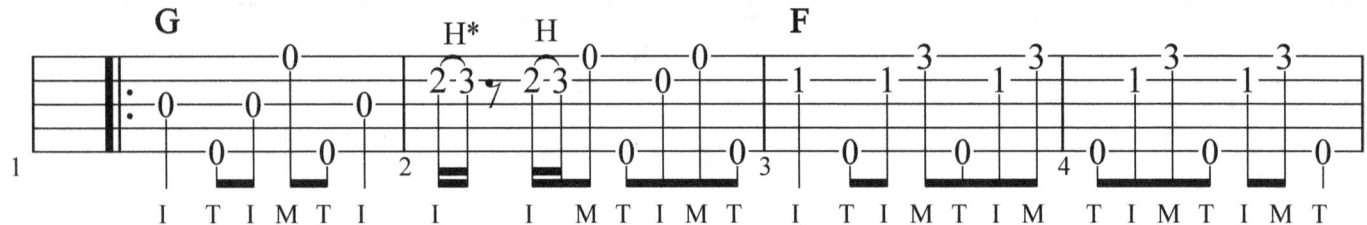

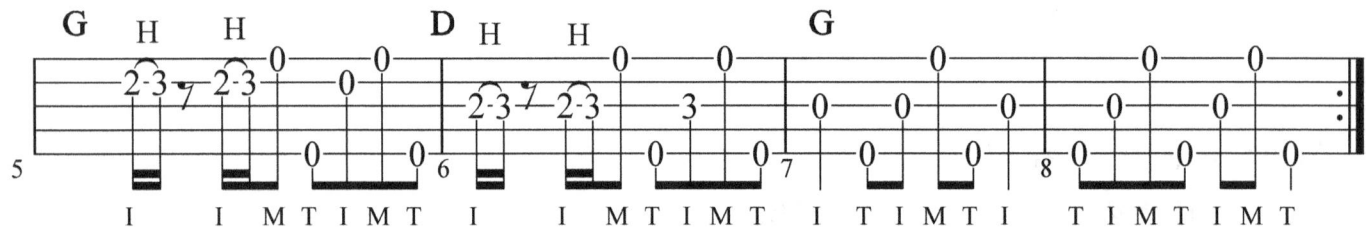

* To review hammer-ons, go to the free lesson entitled "Hammer-ons" at BanjoCompass.com.

**There are four separate .mp3 tracks available for each song so that you can practice at different speeds with a full band. These are available at:

cvls.com/extras/ebs

Little Maggie

Traditional

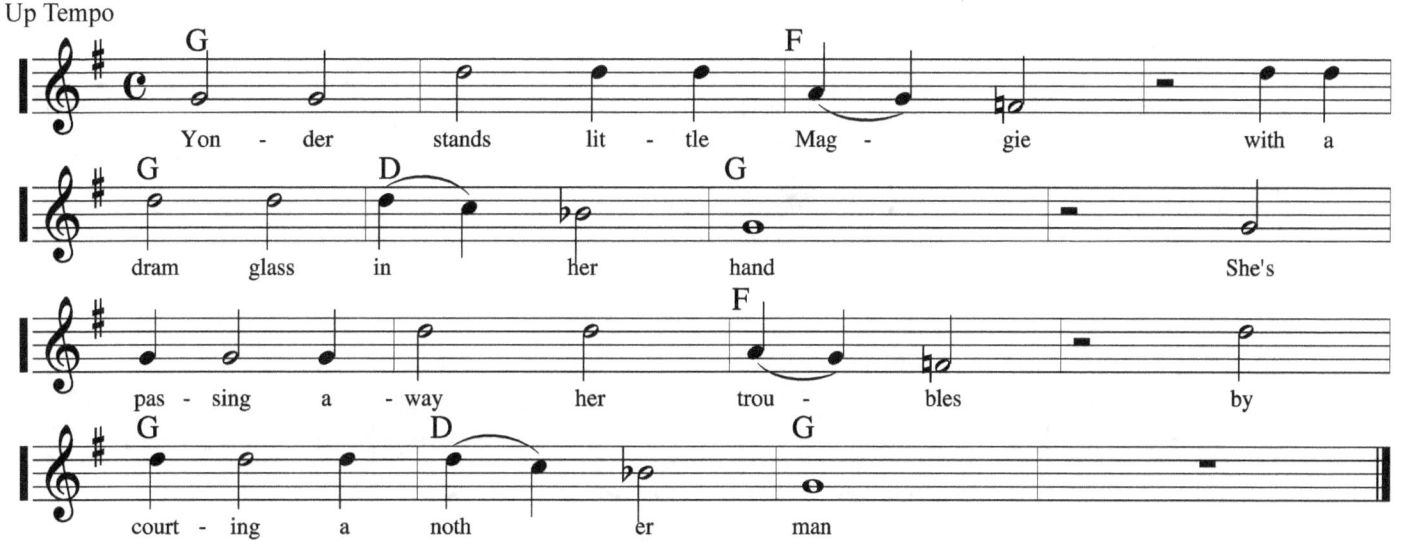

Yonder stands little Maggie with a dram glass in her hand
She's passing away her troubles by courting another man

Oh how can I ever stand it just to see them two blue eyes
Shining in the moonlight like two diamonds in the skies

Pretty flowers were made for blooming, pretty stars were made to shine
Pretty women were made for loving, Little Maggie was made for mine

Last time I saw little Maggie she was setting on the banks of the sea
With a forty-four around her and a banjo on her knee

Lay down your last gold dollar, lay down your gold watch and chain
Little Maggie's gonna dance for Daddy, listen to this old banjo ring

I'm going down to the station with my suitcase in my hand
I'm going away for to leave you, I'm going to some far distant land

Go away, go away little Maggie, go and do the best you can
I'll get me another woman, you can get you another man

Ralph Stanley / Ralph Stanley Plays Requests
Bill Monroe / Bluegrass Ramble
Ricky Skaggs / Bluegrass Rules

Tom Dooley

Traditional

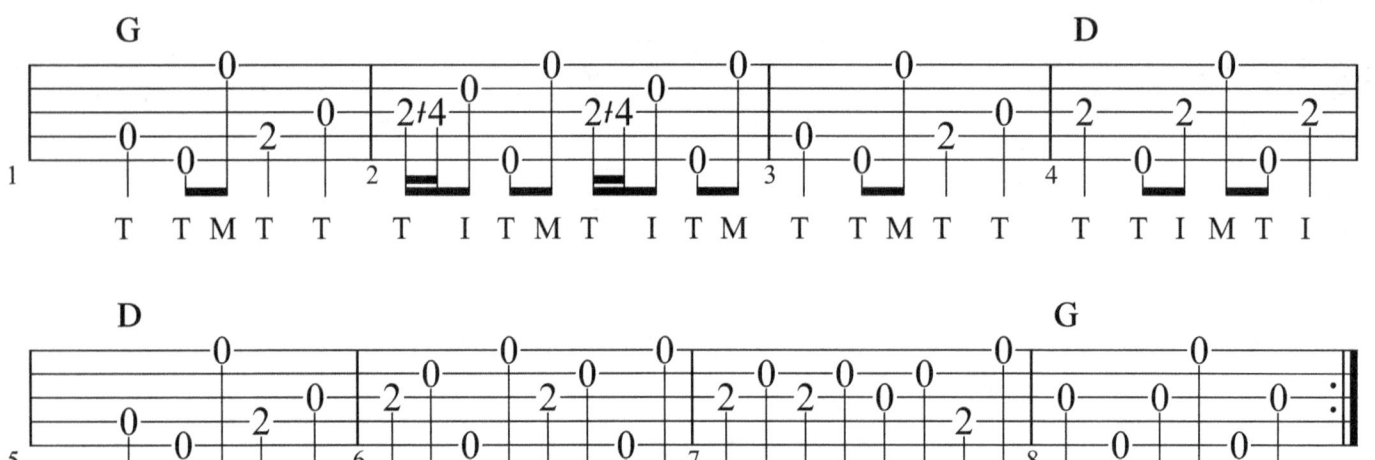

Jam Class - John C. Campbell Folk School 2014

Tom Dooley

Traditional

Chorus
    G
Hang down your head Tom Dooley
Hang down your head and **D** cry
Hang down your head Tom Dooley
Poor boy you're bound to **G** die

I met her on the mountain
There I took her life
I met her on the mountain
Stabbed her with a knife
Chorus

Bout this time tomorrow
Reckon where I'll be
Hadn't of been for Grayson
I'd have been in Tennessee
Chorus

Bout this time tomorrow
Reckon where I'll be
Down in some lonesome canyon
Hanging from a white oak tree
Chorus

Kingston Trio - The Very Best of the Kingston Trio
Grateful Dead - Reckoning - Disc 2
Doc Watson - The Essential Doc Watson

Exercise 1

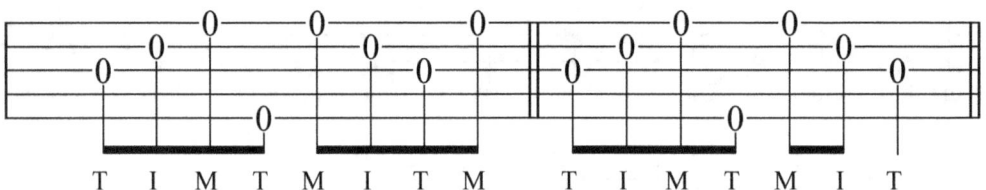

Salty Dog Blues

Traditional

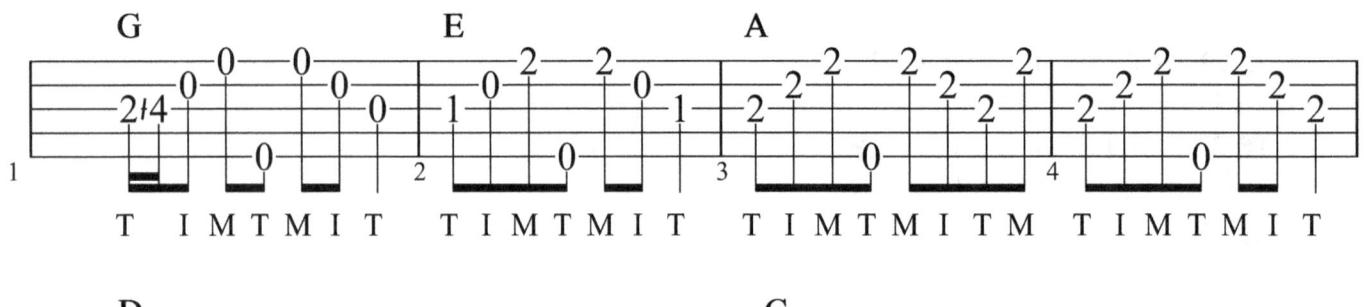

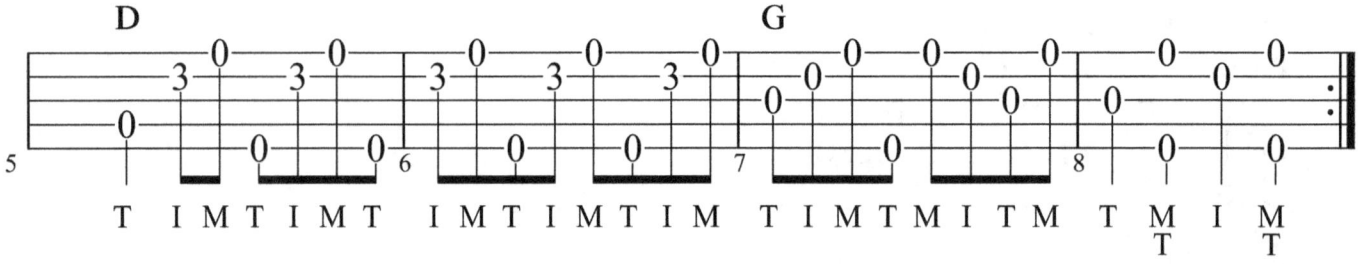

34

Salty Dog Blues

Traditional

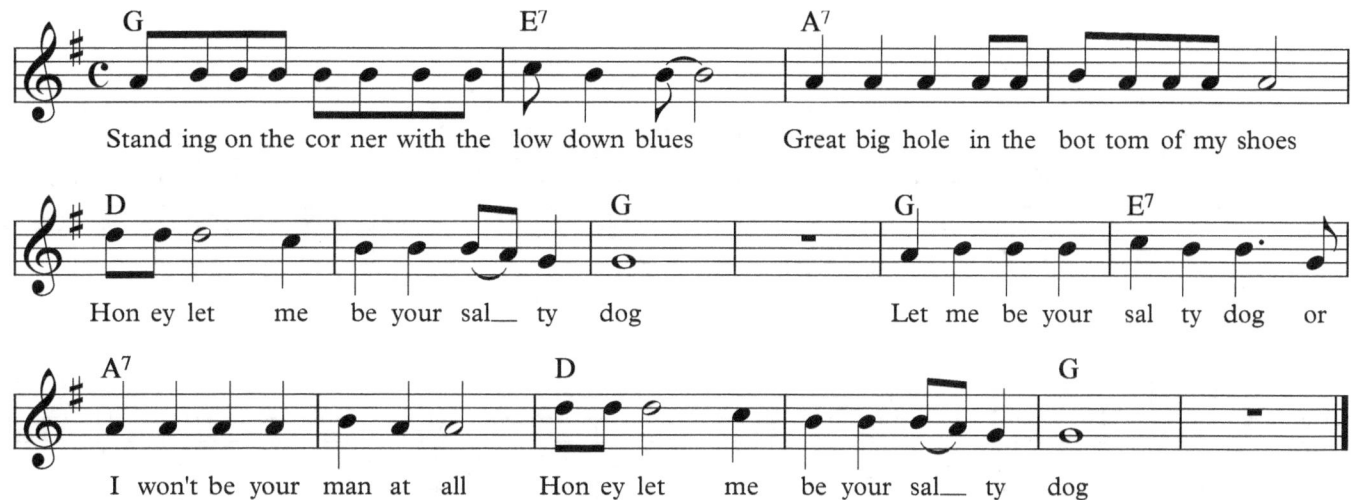

Chorus:
Standing on the corner with the low down blues
Great big hole in the bottom of my shoes
Honey let me be your salty dog
Let me be your salty dog
Or I won't be your man at all
Honey let me be your salty dog

Listen here Sal, well I know you
Rundown stockings and a worn out shoe
Honey me be your salty dog
Chorus

Down in the wildwood sitting on a log
Finger on the trigger and eye on the hog
Honey let me be your salty dog
Chorus

Pulled the trigger and they said go
Shot fell down in Mexico
Honey let me be your salty dog
Chorus

Flatt & Scruggs/The Complete Early Recordings
Allen Brothers/1920s Classics
Doc & Merle Watson/Bear's Sonic Journals

Train 45 - Break 1

Traditional

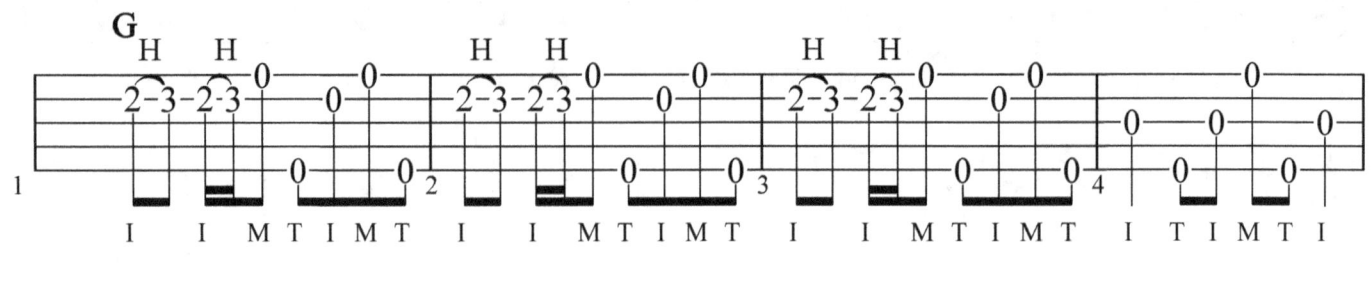
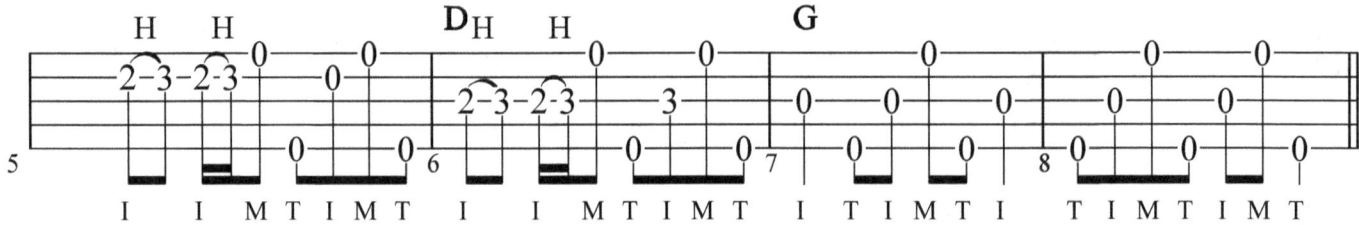

Train 45 - Break 2

Traditional

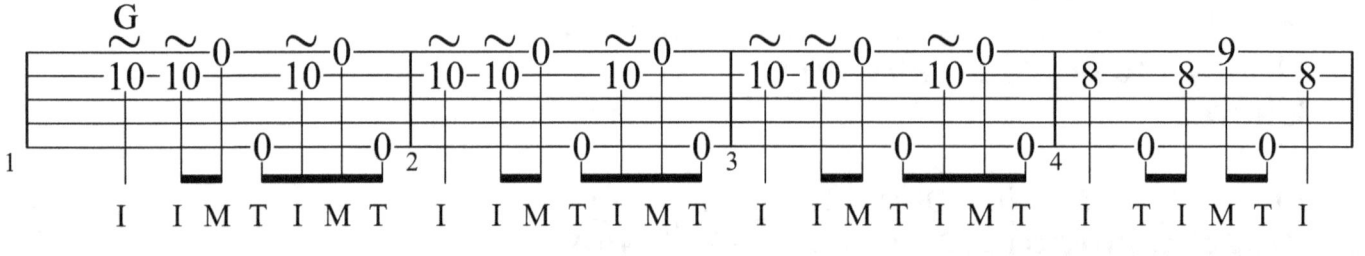
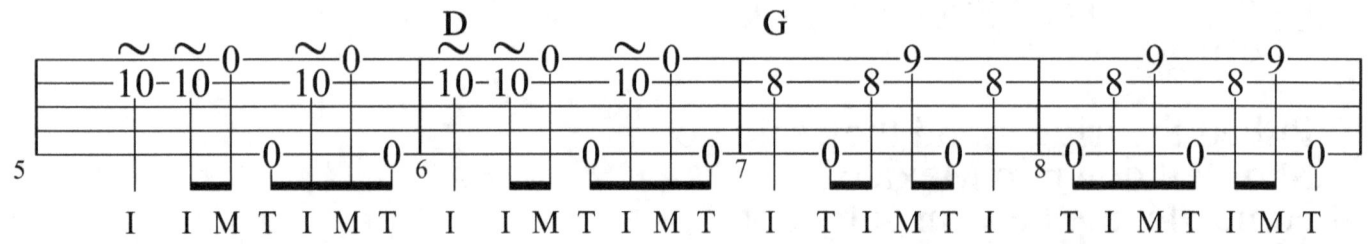

Train 45 - Break 3

Traditional

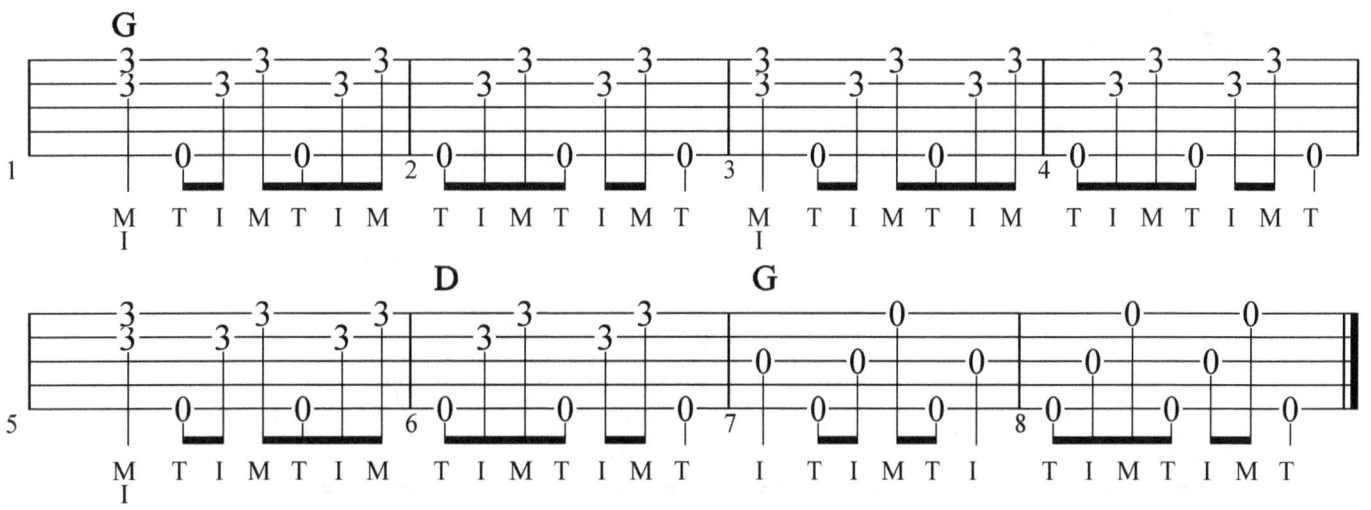

Note: Train 45, Sourwood Mountain, and the remaining four songs in this book are instrumentals, so there are no lyrics.

Sourwood Mountain

Traditional

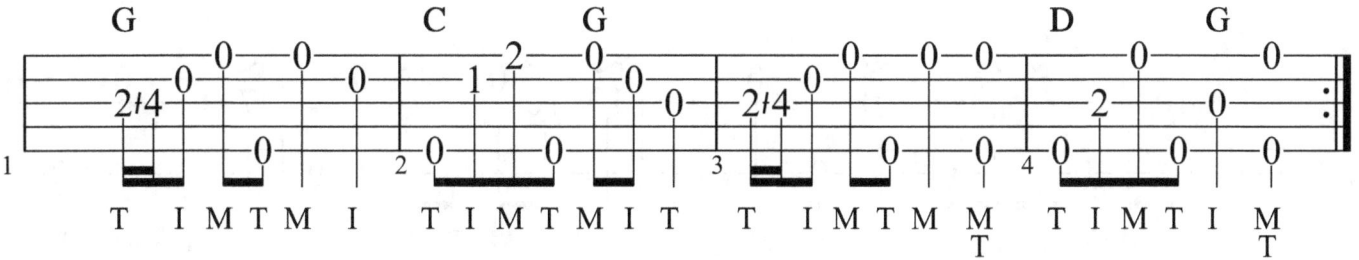

37

Exercise 1

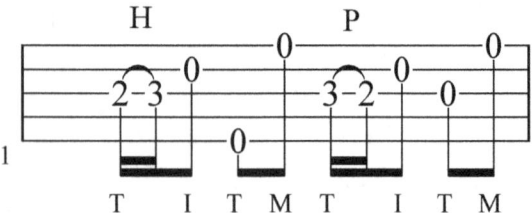

Rueben's Train - Break 1

Traditional

D tuning - See video for tuning instructions

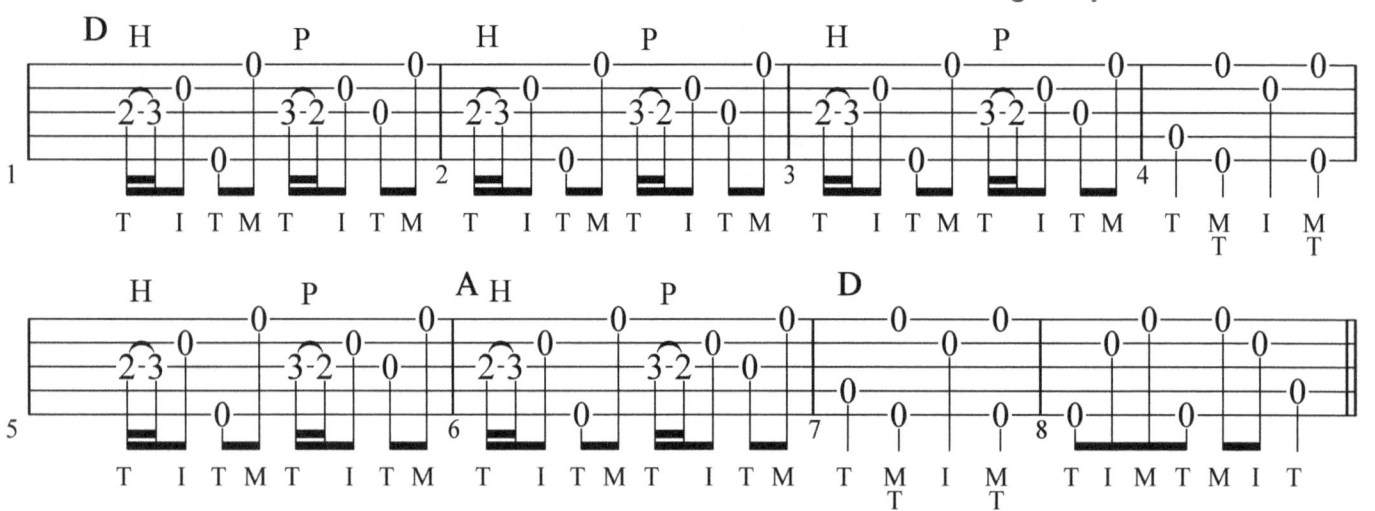

Rueben's Train - Break 2

Traditional

D tuning - See video for tuning instructions

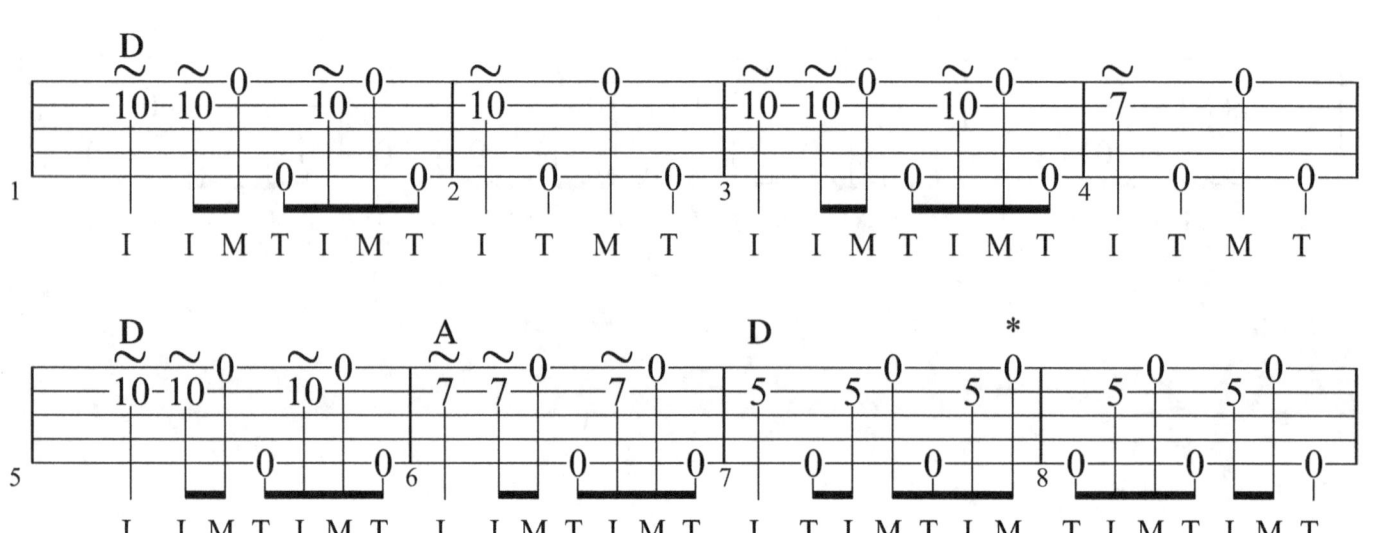

* Optional Note - Some of the tracks and exercises include this note and some don't. Notice how the addition of the note gives you a different sound.

Home Sweet Home

Traditional

C Tuning - See video for tuning instructions.
4th String is tuned down to a C note.

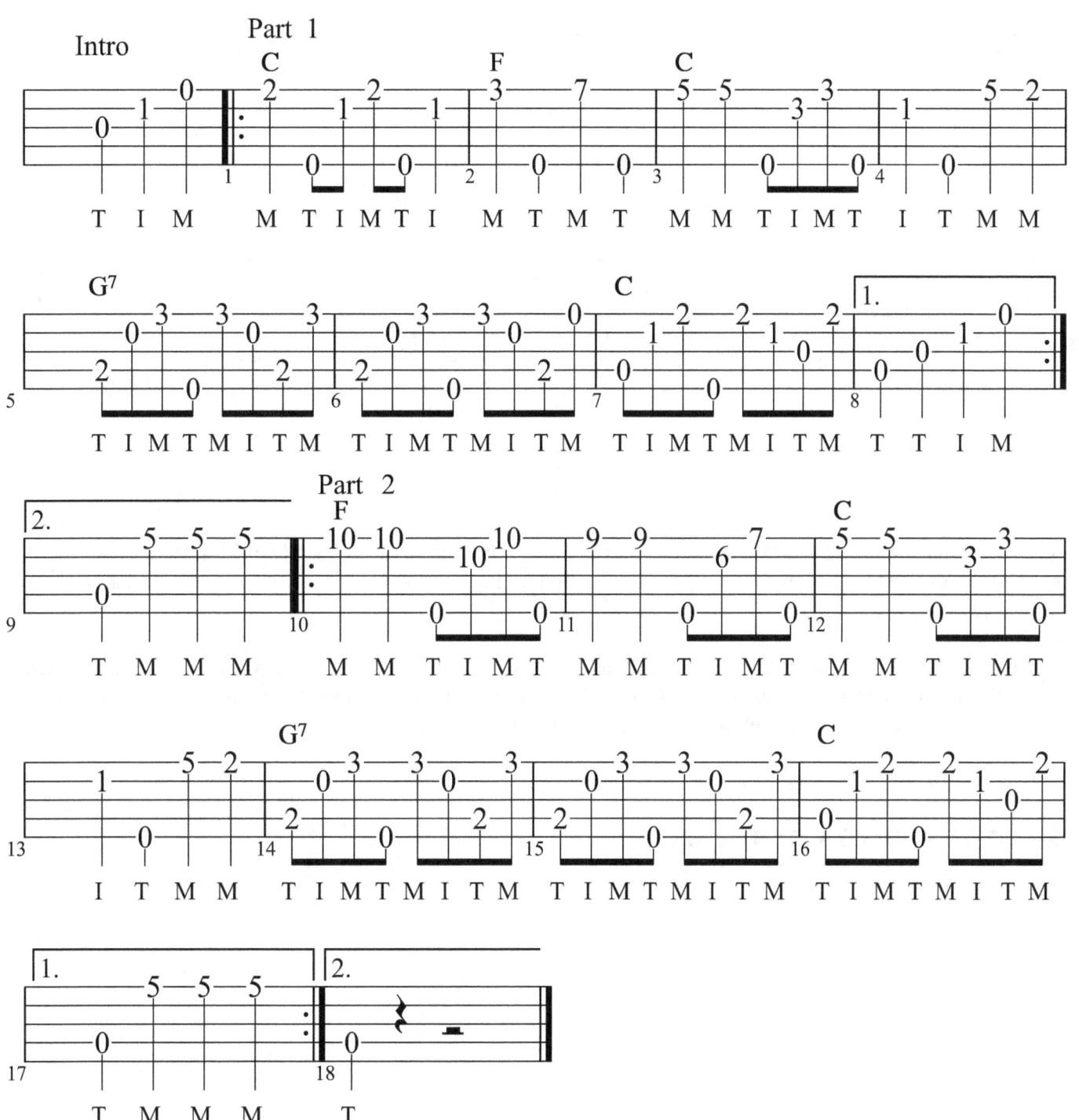

Note: Home Sweet Home was made popular in bluegrass circles by Earl Scruggs and is normally played as an instrumental, so there are no lyrics included.

Arkansas Traveler
Part 1

Traditional

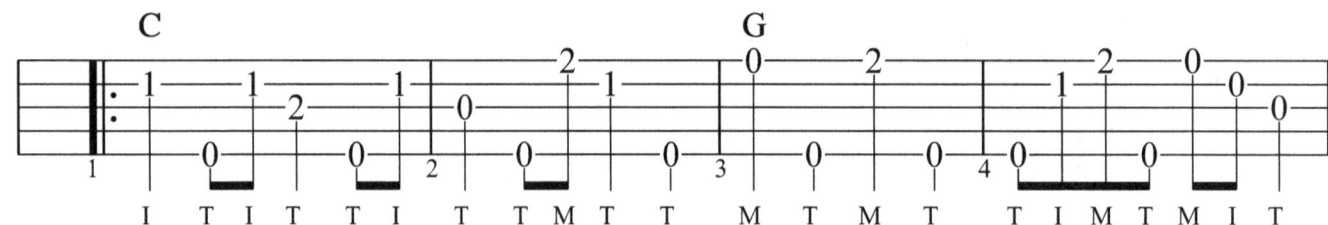

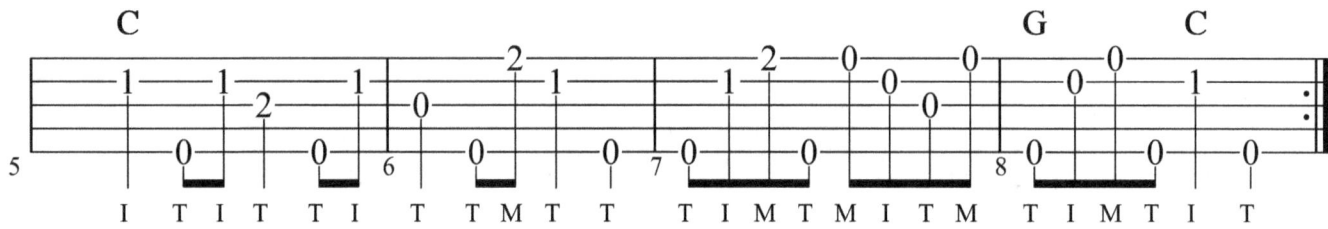

NOTE: This song is played out of C positions and is shown here in the key of C. Most fiddle and mandolin players play this song in the key of D so you would need to use a capo at the 2nd fret to raise your banjo up to the key of D.

Guitar players can play it out of C positions and also use a capo at the 2nd fret for rhythm playing. In this case they would read the chords here as written. It they choose to play it out of "open D" positions they would play this chord progression: (Written below as one beat per letter)

Part 1 |: D D D D   A A A A   D D D D   D D A D :|

Part 2 |: D G D A   D G D A D G D A   D G A D :|

Arkansas Traveler
Part 2

Traditional

*See note on page 40 about chord progressions

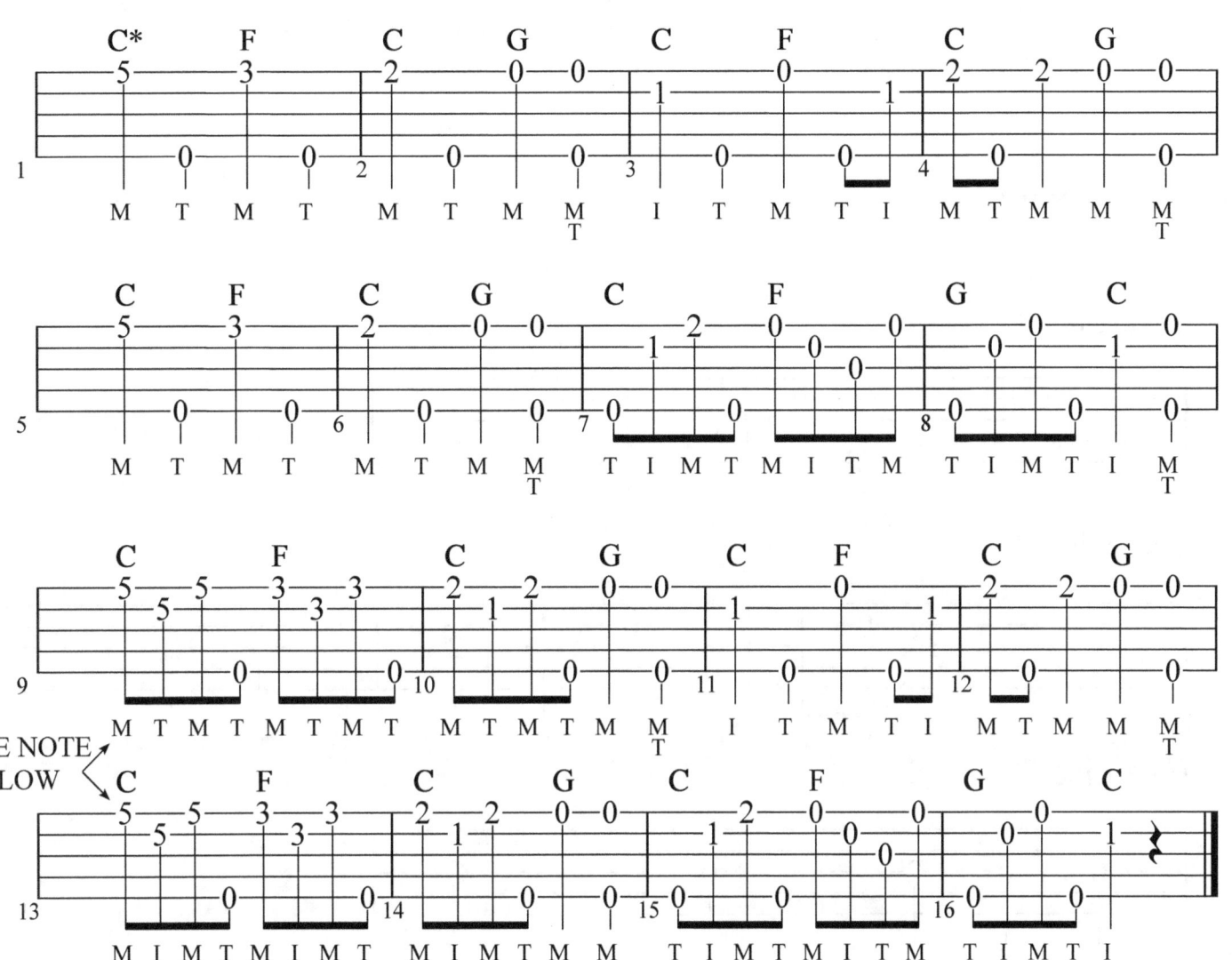

Note: The rolls in measures 9, 10, 13 & 14 can be played either MTMT or MIMT as explained in the video.

Dueling Banjos

Just about everybody has heard the song *Dueling Banjos* that was made popular in the movie *Deliverance*. The song features a call and answer where the guitar plays and the banjo answers or repeats what the guitar just played.

The arrangement you will be learning is divided into A, B, & C parts and an ending. Each of the four parts is broken down into exercises. Start by learning each exercise and playing it over and over along with the video. Once each part is mastered then play the whole song with the video.

Part A - Exercises

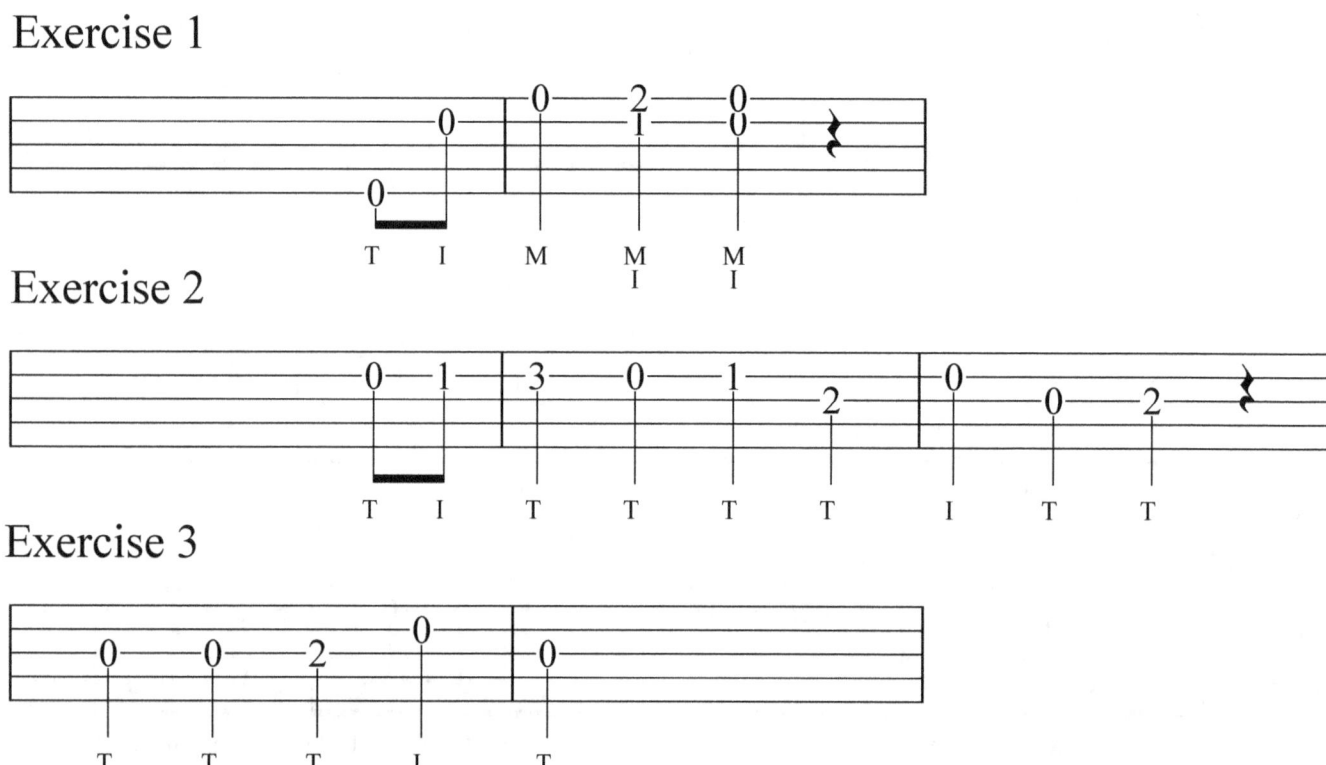

Copyright © 1955 Sony ATV/EMI
Copyright Renewed. All rights reserved.
Used by permission.

Part A - Dueling Banjos

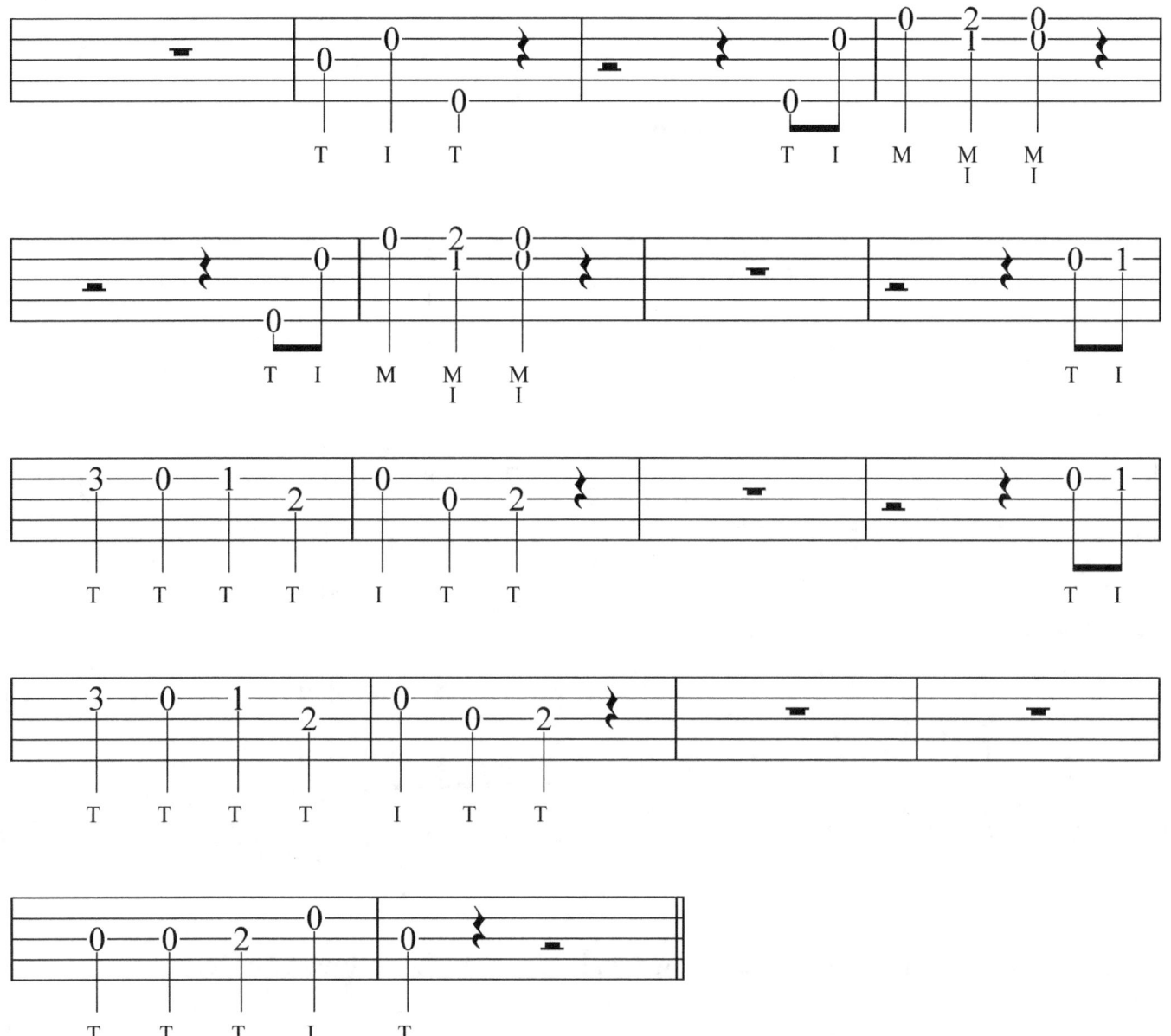

Part B - Exercises

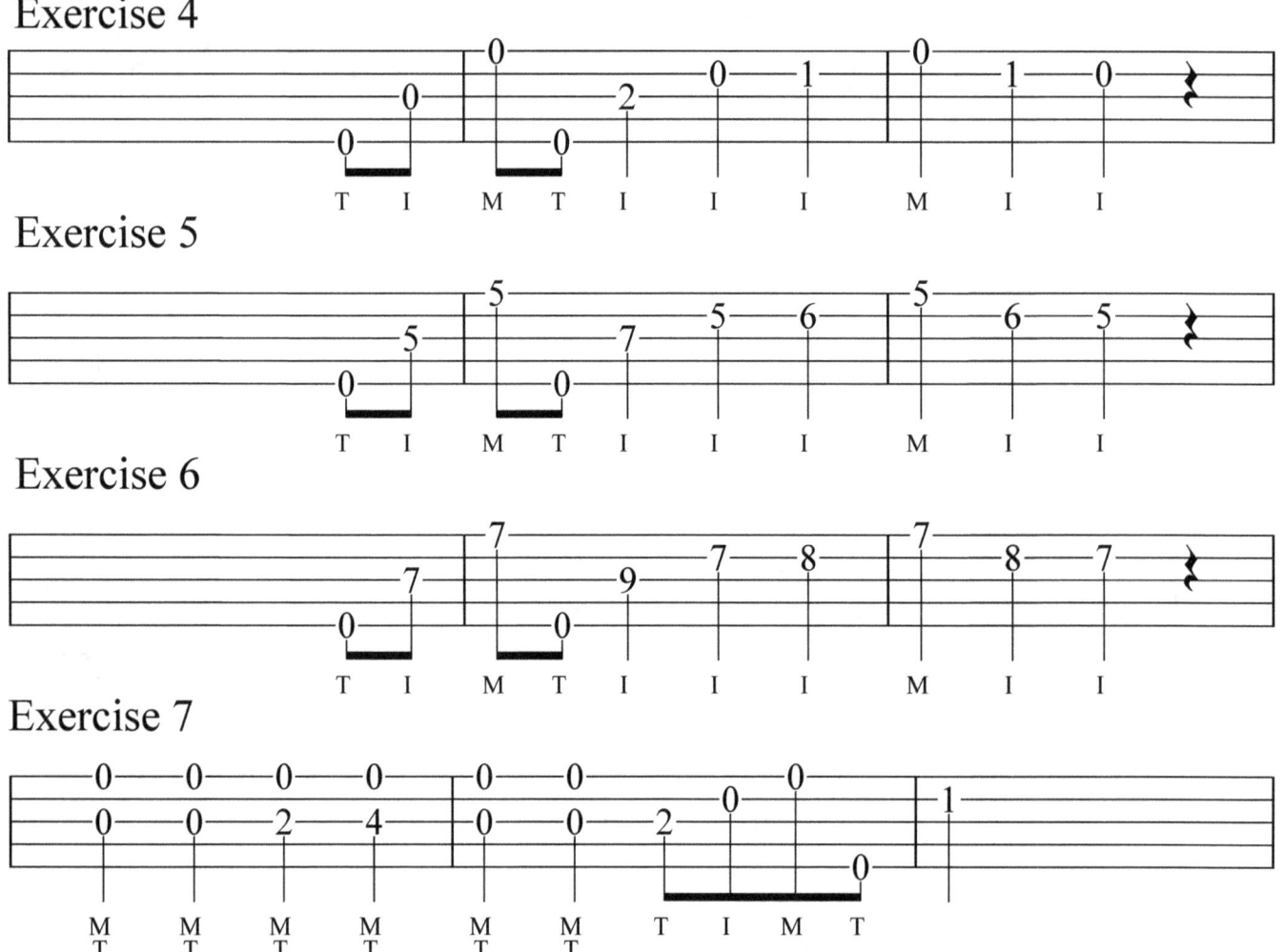

These four exercises are for Part B, which is found on the following page.

Part B - Dueling Banjos

Part C - Exercises

Exercise 8
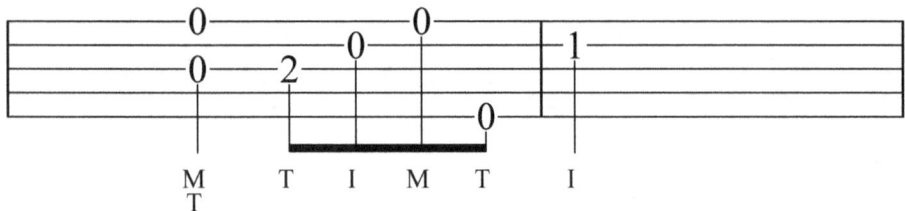

Exercise 9

Exercise 10
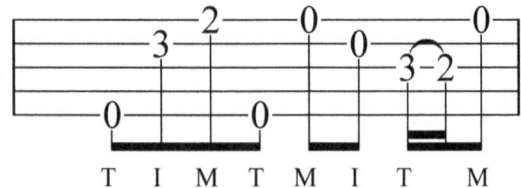

Exercise 11
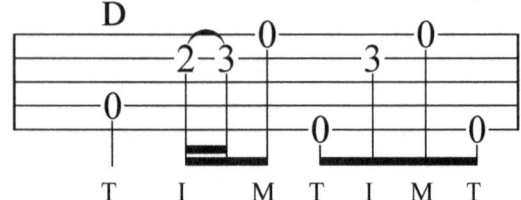

Exercise 12
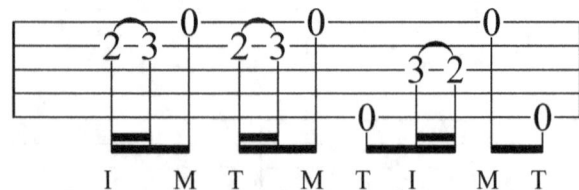

Exercise 13
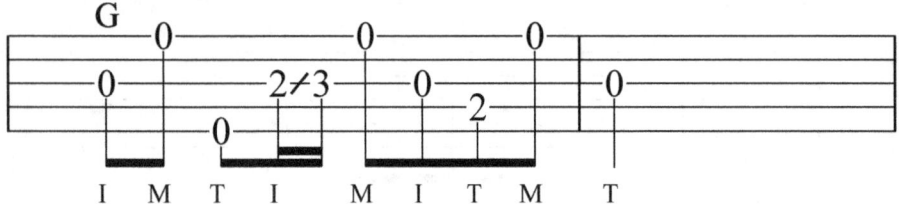

Part C - Dueling Banjos

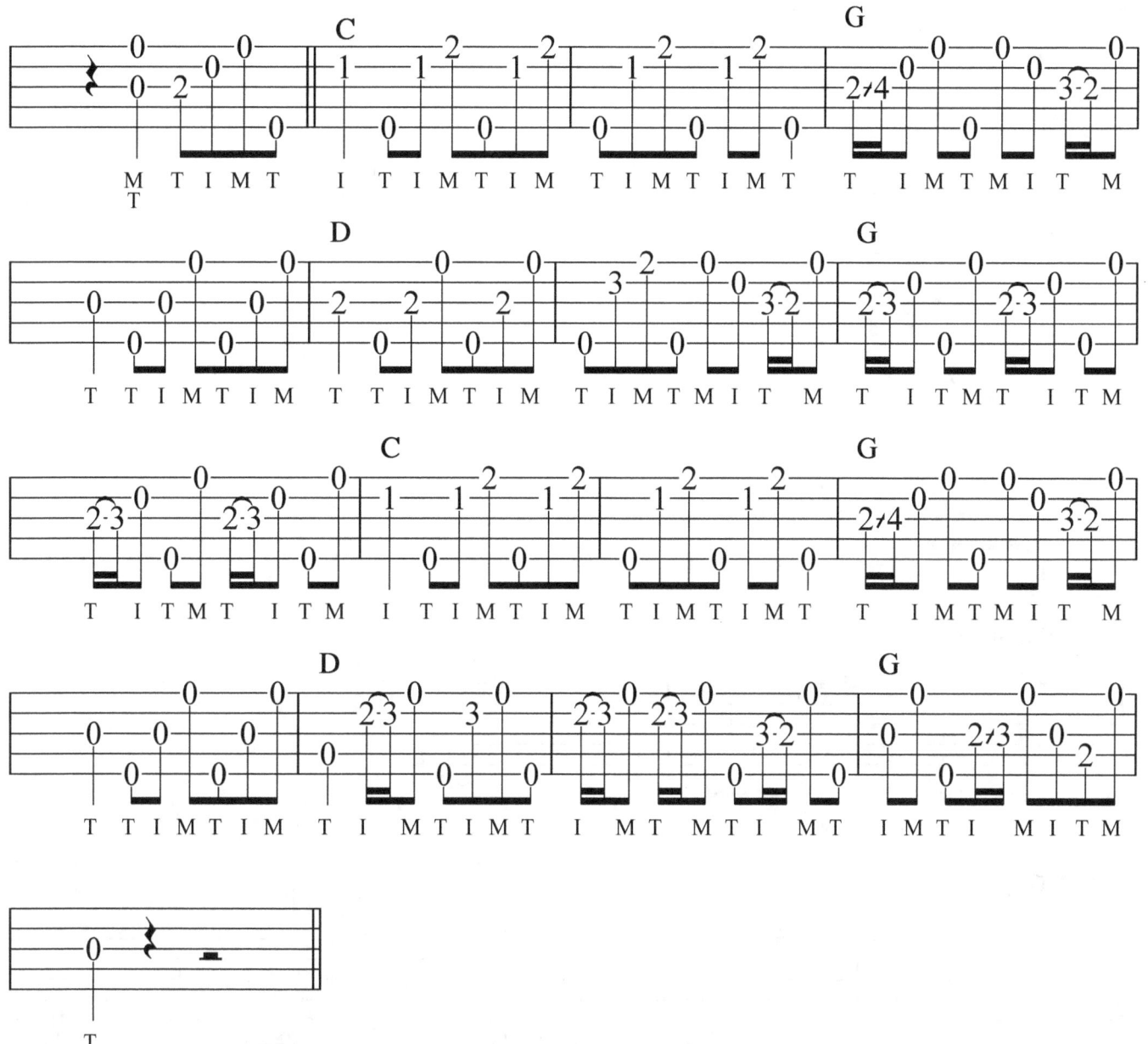

The four exercises for the ending as well as the ending are on the following page.

Ending - Exercises

Exercise 14
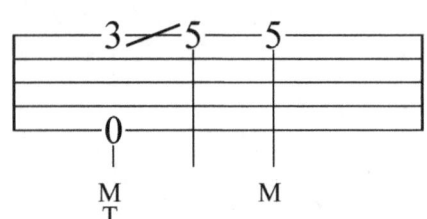

Exercise 15
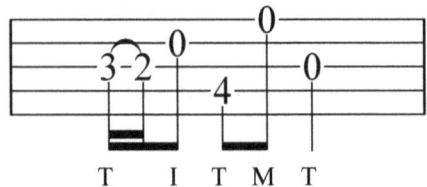

Exercise 16
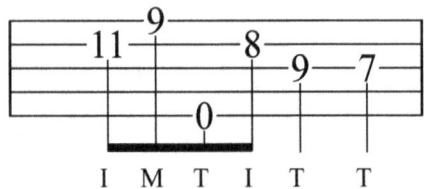

Exercise 17
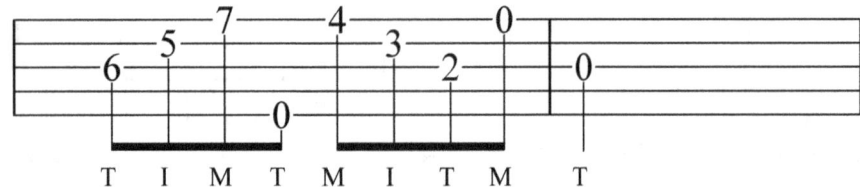

Ending
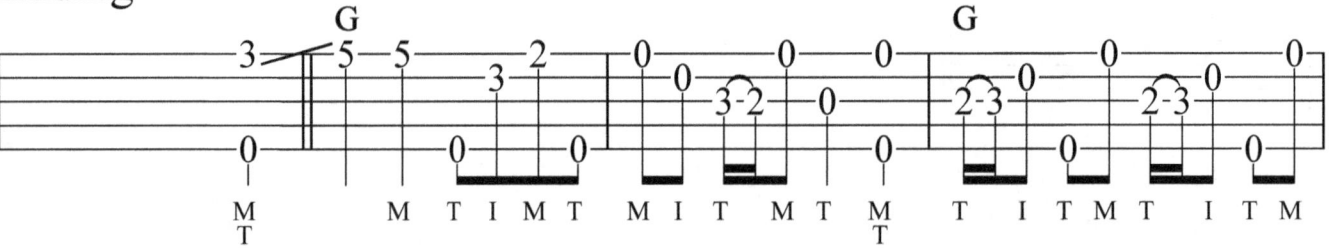
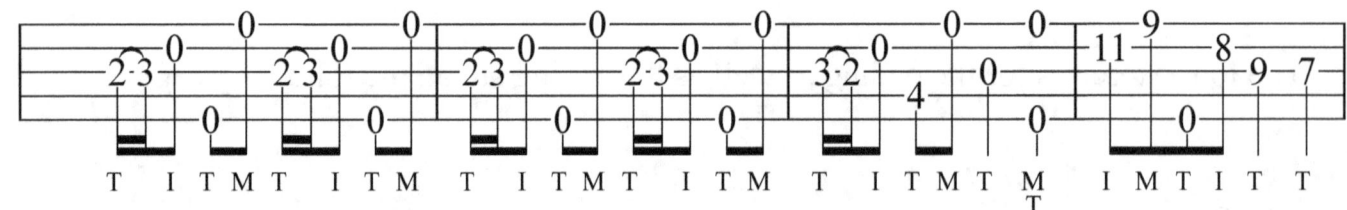
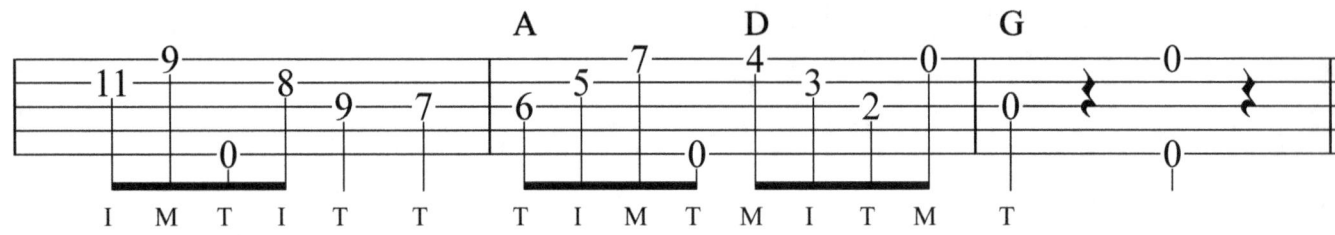

Dueling Banjos
Complete Arrangement

Arranged By Geoff Hohwald

Part A

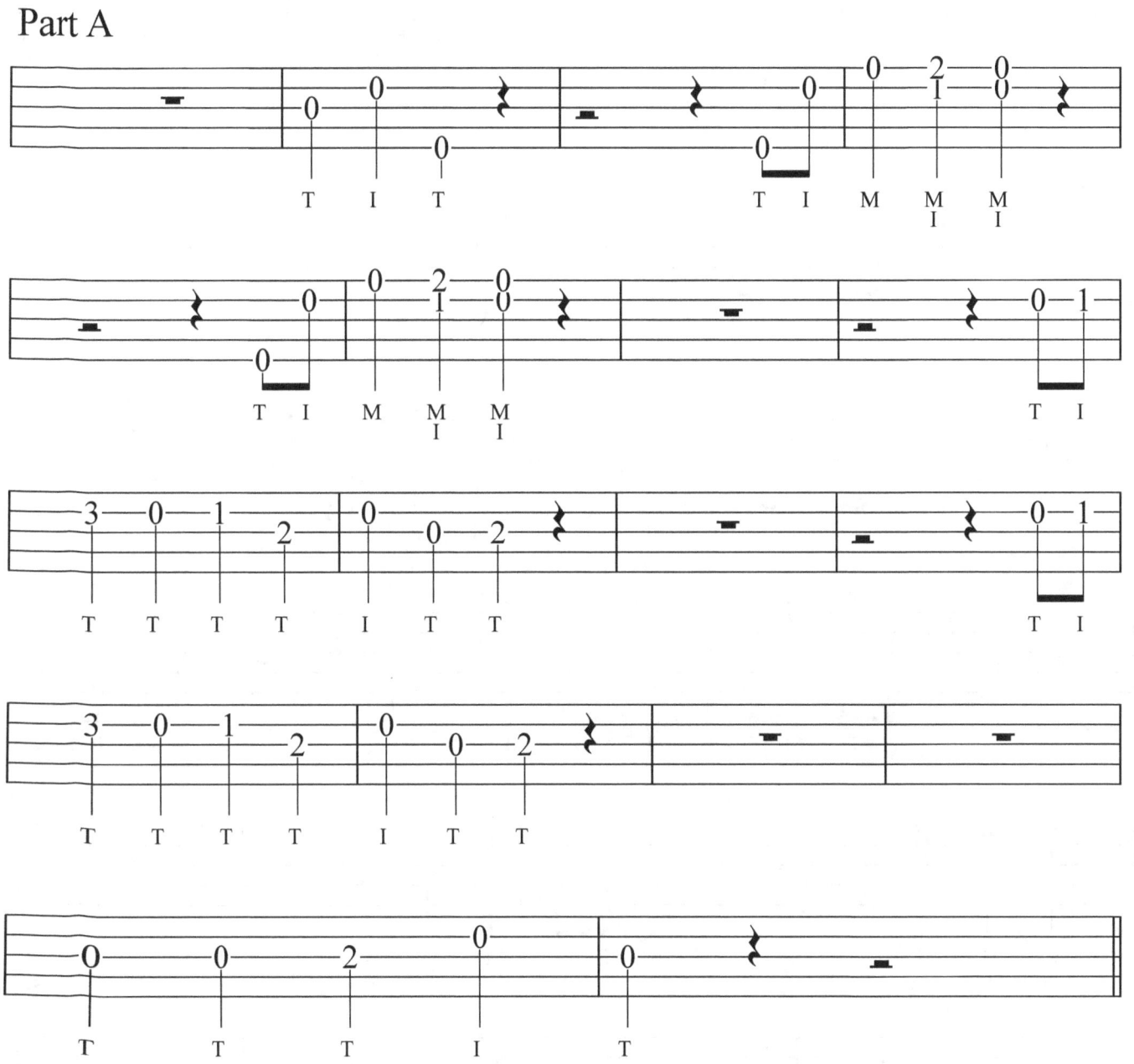

We recommend that you listen to *Dueling Banjos* on the Video several times to get the arrangement in your head.

Copyright © 1955 Sony ATV/EMI
Copyright Renewed. All rights reserved.
Used by permission.

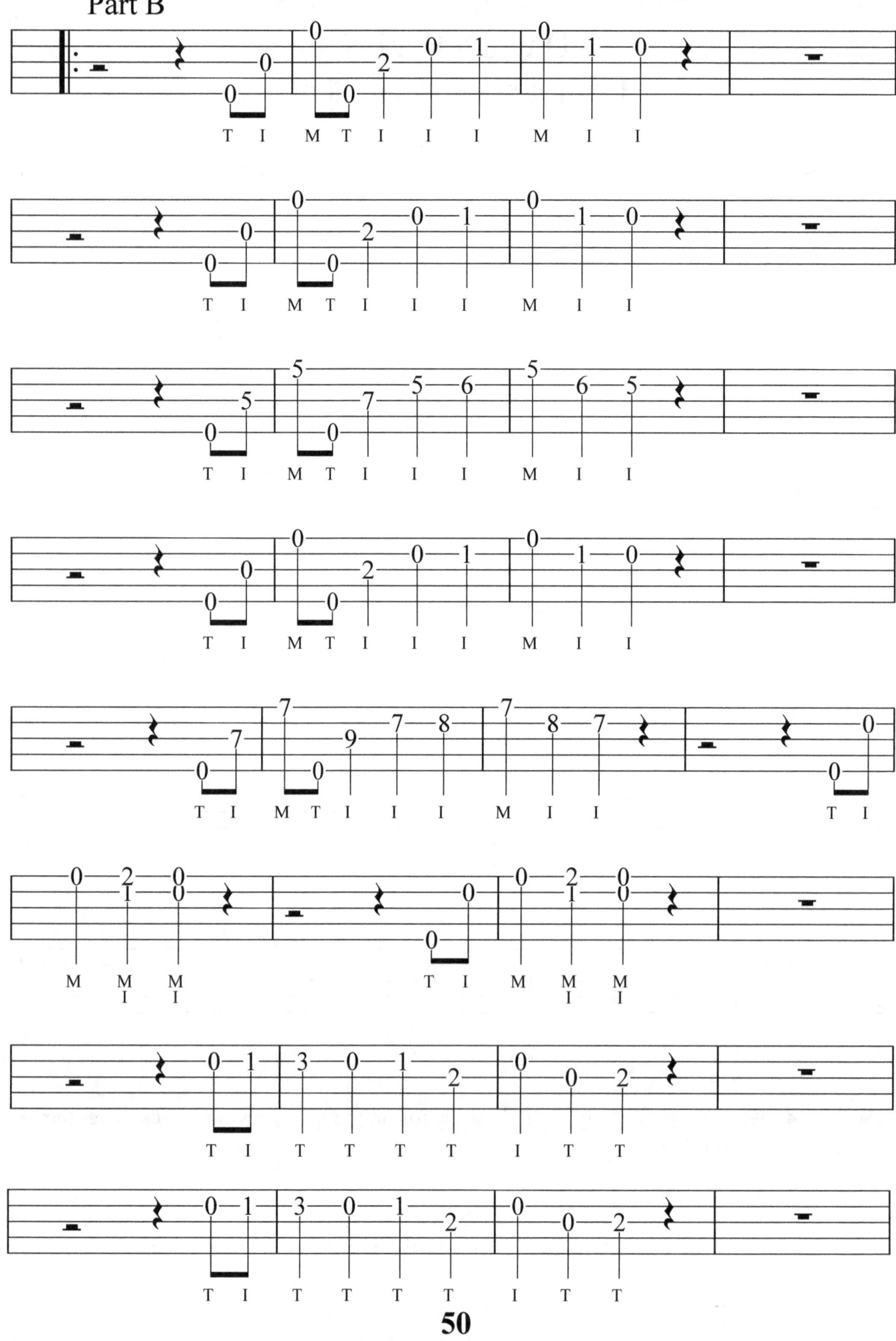

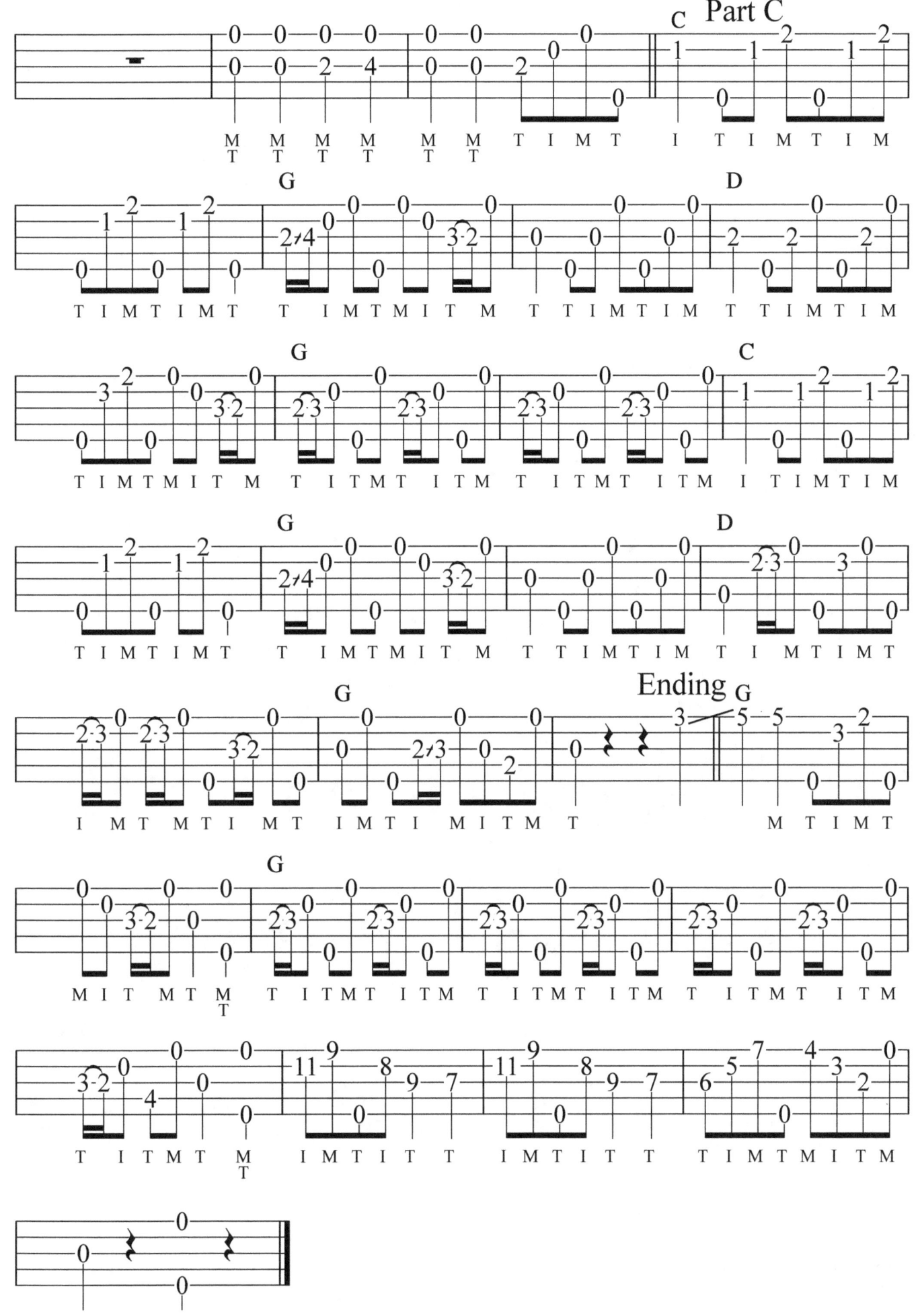